Smart retail

PEARSON
Prentice Hall
BUSINESS

Books that make you better

Books that make you better. That make you *be* better, *do* better, *feel* better. Whether you want to upgrade your personal skills or change your job, whether you want to improve your managerial style, become a more powerful communicator, or be stimulated and inspired as you work.

Prentice Hall Business is leading the field with a new breed of skills, careers and development books. Books that are a cut above the mainstream – in topic, content and delivery – with an edge and verve that will make you better, with less effort.

Books that are as sharp and smart as you are.

Prentice Hall Business.
We work harder – so you don't have to.

For more details on products, and to contact us, visit
www.pearsoned.co.uk
www.yourmomentum.com

RICHARD HAMMOND

Smart retail

How to turn your store into
a sales phenomenon

PEARSON
Prentice Hall
BUSINESS

London • New York • Toronto • Sydney • Tokyo • Singapore
Hong Kong • Cape Town • Madrid • Paris • Amsterdam • Munich • Milan

PEARSON EDUCATION LIMITED

Head Office:
Edinburgh Gate
Harlow CM20 2JE
Tel: +44 (0)1279 623623
Fax: +44 (0)1279 431059
Website: www.pearsoned.co.uk

First published in Great Britain in 2003

© Pearson Education Limited 2003

The right of Richard Hammond to be identified as Author of this Work has been
asserted by him in accordance with the Copyright, Designs and Patents Act 1988.

ISBN-10: 0-273-67521-4
ISBN-13: 978-0-273-67521-1

British Library Cataloguing in Publication Data
A CIP catalogue record for this book can be obtained from the British Library

10 9 8 7 6 5

Cover concept by Sarah Ann Smith
Typeset by Northern Phototypesetting Co. Ltd, Bolton
Printed and bound in Great Britain by Bell & Bain Ltd, Glasgow

The Publishers' policy is to use paper manufactured from sustainable forests.

Smart retail

Picture: Koworld

... is dedicated to customers – the people who pay our wages.

Contents

Preface

Retail is physically and mentally hard work. People outside of our business find that hard to accept. We retailers are always under pressure from the bank or the boss. It doesn't matter if you have been in the job ten minutes or ten years; the pressure is *always* there. Every day could be a disaster or a triumph. When we make things go well, when the team clicks, when customers open their hearts and wallets, when the store feels right; those days, that magic, is what keeps us coming back for more.

Welcome then to *Smart Retail*, where together we can ensure that you enjoy more days of triumph, better profits, a happier team, an improved business performance and a boost to your retail career. I love selling things in shops, it is my passion and when we get that right and delighted customers happily hand us their money, wow that feels good.

Why simple is great

The essence of this book is about helping you to make more money, to win the sales battle, to help you and your team stand out from among the UK's 322,101 shops. Much of what I am going to talk you through has been done before. I make no secret of that. You will already know lots of it and you will easily understand all of it. What is new is twofold. First never have so many simple things been gathered together in one easy-to-use book, and second some of the ways of applying these simple things are absolutely new. Together these two factors offer you a chance to grab competitive advantage in your market place and in your retail career.

Stars of the shop floor

A good chain-store manager, or owner, can make a huge impact on the success of a retail shop, much more so than a high-flying marketing director or clever finance chief. With a good manager at the helm, great sales people, assistants and administrators can also make a big and immediate impact. The ideas in this book are so accessible that any member of the team can use them to achieve something special, to help boost business performance.

Your motivation for reading *Smart Retail* might be to earn better bonuses, to boost your self-esteem, to accelerate your retail career or to keep the bank happy. My motivation is to try to make a tough job just a little bit easier. The ideas, strategies and techniques covered here are a distillation of the best in the world. I have spent time with the UK's best, the USA's best and learned too from excellent stores in Japan, Spain, France and Germany.

The ideas, strategies and techniques covered here are a distillation of the best in the world.

I'm hoping that you will read *Smart Retail*, apply some of the ideas and enjoy improved business performance, but for some readers this experience will lead to more than just extra sales and profit. Some people, and I hope that might be you, will read this book and a light will go on, they will see more clearly than ever before that they are special. That they can achieve anything they want to in this business. It's been fun writing this book but if just one person, maybe you, uses *Smart Retail* to realise better their real potential, then that is what will give me the biggest reward.

We are entering a retail era in which the merchants, those who have served on the front-line in the stores, are back in charge. That is very good news for you. Whatever your current position in the company, store manager, new assistant, or experienced area manager, there is nothing to stop you taking the plunge and surging ahead in your career. Nothing to stop you from running the company one day. If you have passion and energy, if you like people and you value the pleasure you are delivering to customers then you are in with a real chance. If you already own a single store, then there is nothing stopping you from taking on the big players and winning, nothing to stop you from adding new stores to that successful first one. Indeed the tools you need are all right here.

There has never been a better time to accelerate your retail career. In the UK 4.4m people work in shops. Everybody else, without exception, shops. In other words, millions of us earn our wages from retail and all of us use retail. So crucial is retail that American Presidents down the years have urged their people to shop the country's way out of recession. Here at home the strength of our retail sector, the one you are an important part of, is credited by economists as the reason why Britain escaped the turn of the century recessions that hit Germany, France, Japan and the US.

Good retailers, at all levels, are in demand as never before. You are reading *Smart Retail* at absolutely the right time – now! Wages, conditions, challenges and opportunities are opening up fast. Single stores have become multi-million pound businesses. Even village convenience stores can be turning seven figure revenues. Chain-store managers in the big out-of-town sheds can be earning more than accountants, management consultants, or civil servants. Indeed at Home Depot (an American store that's a lot like B&Q) in 2002 the average general store manager earned an annual salary of $150,000. This is a wonderful time for you to have chosen to boost your retail career.

Now, let's get down to business!

Acknowledgements

A retail career takes us away from our family and friends for huge chunks of time. To be a retailer is impossible without the dedicated support of the people we love. I have been lucky to have a wonderful family who support me in all those twists and turns that a life in retail offers.

I would like to say thank you to those inspirational friends who have made retail so rewarding for me. First to Umesh Vadodaria and Mahendra Patel for making me get off my bum and do things. To 'Buffalo' Steve Smith for that very first break at 16. To Glyn Moser for making me see how important people are. To Janet for the belief that I could get the things in my head out and down on paper. To Graeme for saying that my writing wasn't completely rubbish. To Rachael Stock at Pearson for making this book better than I had imagined it could be. Thank you also to all the many retailers who gave up time, advice and ideas for *Smart Retail* – you know who you are and you are all superstars. And to Monkey for all the tea and smiles.

I would like to add this last thing. All the effort, sacrifice, set-backs and challenges have been worth it. Retail is the best life in the world.

Introduction

To make this book easier to read I have pitched *Smart Retail* from the store manager's perspective but all retail roles will get the full benefit from reading the book. So to help you get the best from *Smart Retail* I've written some notes below that are specific to your job role. Have a look at these before you plunge into the main parts. There are four main parts:

1 **You** – *making things happen.*
2 **People** – *you and your team.*
3 **Customer** – *those who pay our wages.*
4 **Store** – *the Aladdins' caves.*

Each part can be read in any order, or even on its own. You might want to start with whichever area you feel needs most work? It is fair to say that I believe most solutions to retail challenges can be found from within the team, which is why I've put the *People* part near the beginning. Non-managers though might want to skip *People* and read that part last. It's up to you.

Product of course is the umbrella under which everything else sits, so rather than split out product from the rest of the book I have integrated product issues; ranging, selection, pricing and so on throughout *Smart Retail*.

Above all this is a working book. I invite you to flick through, to cherry-pick the bits that suit you best, scribble on the pages, tear stuff out and share it. If I ever came into your store I would love to see that your copy of the book had a broken spine, page corners turned down, a forest of post-it notes sticking out of the top, and coffee stains on the cover.

Your job and *Smart Retail*

Store manager

Most of you who manage but do not own stores, will be working for a chain. If that's a small chain you will have lots of opportunity to influence important aspects of the store. You may be able to persuade an owner to introduce new lines or to run certain promotions. If that's the case you can read this book as an owner.

You may instead be one manager out of a hundred, or out of six hundred for that matter. It can feel really hard sometimes to get your voice heard. As you read the book you'll see that I make lots of suggestions on how to increase your company profile and on how to get your ideas actioned.

In most cases I've made practical suggestions for ensuring take-up of your ideas. You'll also find that pretty much all *Smart Retail* ideas and strategies include suggestions covering the effective steps you can take without needing to ask permission from someone else first. All of the sections on people management can be applied right away in your store without having to request additional resources and are in line with most company's current rules in these areas.

Store owner

You are in a fantastic position – you are able to vary any aspect of your business that you want to. You can choose to buy new ranges, change the name of the store, pay for promotions, invest in new equipment and so on. You have free reign in this book. Sometimes you do need to spend money on your business, especially on the site itself. However I am a strong believer in the notion that many things you might need to do, can be done very cheaply indeed, but without looking cheap to either customers or colleagues.

As is the case for the chain-store manager, all of the advice and ideas on people management can be applied directly for free, and are presented in a practical and obvious way. This means that either you or the managers you employ can make a significant positive impact on the business right away without spending a penny.

Franchisee

Yours is a situation that sits between store owner and store manager. You own, manage and promote the business but you do so within well-controlled guidelines. Franchising is a great opportunity for good retailers and

Smart Retail offers you many ideas and strategies that are also appropriate in a good franchise.

Team member

There are lots of different reasons why we go into retail, let's be honest those reasons might include necessity and convenience. I think though, that you might just be in it for better reasons. After all you have bought, or are considering buying, a book on retail; you are getting hooked by the business. That makes you very important to me. This book is the tool that will help you to make the most of, and accelerate, your retail career. Use it to make suggestions in team meetings, use it to develop your management style and your leadership skills.

> **This book is the tool that will help you to make the most of, and accelerate, your retail career.**

Many of the parts and chapters in *Smart Retail* deal with the fundamentals of retail, a good knowledge of these will make you very attractive to employers as you progress your career. To help you get the complete picture it really is worth, just once, going through the whole book from beginning to end.

As you read try to consider things from a store manager's point of view. By doing that you will find it much easier to pitch your ideas to your actual manager. I've also built some of the action plans in a way that means you can easily adapt them to make great interview presentations. Especially useful when you are chasing promotion or applying for a job with a new team.

Assistant store manager (ASM)

You are the backbone of retail management, without good ASMs many stores just do not work. I hope you are alongside a good manager. If you are that person will value your input and it will be easy for you to make *Smart Retail* work your way. Luckily most of you will be working in good teams and for good people so use this opportunity to make some positive noise. Make good use of the planning tools provided here and you will gain lots from *Smart Retail*.

Area manager

Yours is a tricky job and you probably don't need me to tell you that. Nevertheless, as one of the few people in the company that sees lots of stores but also spends time in central offices with the senior team you are in a unique position. You have the opportunity to make a big impact on the overall success of the business.

It is a pressure role and *Smart Retail* can help you to deliver ideas and strategies that keep your boss happy, and that can help you to feel that you are actually moving the business forward. You are one of the audiences that I put most thought into when constructing the book, as a result there are three options for progressing ideas that I would like to I recommend you choose from:

1   Take a single idea and then apply it across all your stores at the same time. This ensures everyone is focused on a single shared goal.

2   Draw up a plan across the area featuring all the ideas and strategies you would like to use. Test different ideas in separate stores at the same time, and then roll out only those ideas that you have seen work best.

3   Use the *People* part on its own to help each of your managers create great cultures in their stores. This alone will dramatically improve sales and profit

Central functions (marketing, sales operations, administration and so on)

If you started your retail career at the coalface in a shop, then you will really enjoy reading *Smart Retail*. Many of the stories and ideas will bring back some, hopefully, good memories. Other sections could well act as useful updates to your experience.

If you have never worked in a shop, then *Smart Retail* is the best look into the in-store reality you could ever hope for. No matter how good your ad agency is, there is no substitute for a proper understanding of what life in-store is really like. *Smart Retail* will give you that.

If you are the sort who feels a study visit to the Whitechapel Road street-market is beneath you, then this book is not for you. On the other hand if you are desperate to find effective ways to gain new competitive advantage, to improve customer service quality or to build better teams then this may just prove to be the best few pounds you'll ever invest.

Notes for all readers

Above all *Smart Retail* is a practical proposition. You don't have to read the whole thing or slavishly follow directions as though they were the ingredients and instructions for making a cake. Just pick out today the one thing that you know can make a difference, then another tomorrow and another the day after. Before very long you will find that these baby steps have begun to add up to a significant journey of change and improvement.

PART ONE – **YOU**

Let's get down to business

Picture: Koworld

Choose your own direction

1

Rolling snowballs and reading stores

Every change has to start somewhere. How do you find that one small thing that can get you on the road to big performance improvement? The good news is that you don't have to change lots of things all in one go to make a difference. Change is about understanding how to see all those fixable faults and good ideas in such a way that you can then pick out just one thing to try today.

One thing changed can be the start of something big. Change one detail that one customer notices, who mentions it to five others, who each tell five more, and you can see that one change can make a big impact. Your team too begins to see things starting to happen, just from one idea. Employee attitudes begin to improve. Baby steps: do one thing brilliantly today, another tomorrow and maybe change the world next week. Remember rolling snowballs as a kid? It's like that. You start small and with a bit of effort you soon have something big going on.

> **Baby steps: do one thing brilliantly today, another tomorrow and maybe change the world next week.**

Too many successes are prevented from happening because a good person cannot make space or time to find that first small change. It's easy to become hidebound by the realities around you. Learning to systematically read a store is an excellent way to break out of that particular rut. You already know how to read a store but you have probably never seen how to use that ability to identify opportunities.

There is an art to reading a store. I should warn you, once you learn to do it systematically shopping is never the same again. You won't even be able to go into a jumble sale without analyzing the store, the people and the customers. So what's the secret? Well that's it: the store, the people and the customers. You need to discover facts about each and then consider how this new knowledge might impact your own business.

Store

I'll bet good money that you already do this when you walk into a store: you look around. You look at the fixtures, the offers, the dirt on the carpet and you spot the display gaps. You might even suck your teeth a bit and feel relieved that some other manager is under pressure for once.

Now stand still and observe

Watch where customers are going.
- Which part of each section do they enter first?

Look at peoples' eyes.
- What do they see?
- What do they miss?

What things do they touch?
- Which items do they pick-up and from where?
- How long do customers linger over each display fixture?

How many lookers at each display take something to the counter, or to the changing room?

What sorts of people are shopping in the store? Mums with pushchairs, office workers or mechanics? (This profile will be different at different times of the day.)

Pay special regard to what happens in the transition zone, that area near the door that transfers customers from the outside and then into the store – how do people move through this area?

Most of us make a really basic mistake when we shop our own store. We tend to look at it from back to front. We usually see the store from the back staff area or warehouse through the shopfloor and out of the front doors. It's a natural mistake but so wrong and very unhelpful. That pillar we hate might actually be acting as a superb natural customer traffic brake when you see from the door in. It might just pay to move some feature merchandise next to that pillar, something tempting and quick to pick-up (usual shoplifter considerations still apply).

Then take a look at the basic store components

▶ Promotions

▶ Range

▶ Pricing logic

▶ Fixtures and fittings

▶ Lighting layouts

▶ Added-value ideas (*see* Chapter 8 for a list of these).

Go through this in your competitor's stores. I believe firms should not only encourage you to go out reading your competitors' stores but that they should even give you a paid session, every week, to go off and do so. In fact they should even give you a fiver to go get a latte to slurp while you walk around, improving your business through learning from your competitors and other retailers.

People

Talk to staff every time you go into a shop. An easy icebreaker is to ask 'What's it like working here?' You will usually get a plain answer along the lines of 'It's not too bad', which doesn't tell you much but does give you a chance to then ask 'What do you like about it?' Nearly every time you ask that the assistant will let slip a nugget of useful information:

▶ There's a nice team spirit.

▶ The pay is good.

▶ It's a laugh.

▶ We're treated with a bit of respect.

▶ Everyday is different.

▶ I like customers.

Each of those answers allows you to unobtrusively ask further questions that help to get to specific employment practices in play at that store. Try to chat with the store manager too. Tell them what you do. Share some thoughts and ideas with them and they often will with you.

Customers

Listen

▶ What do customers say to each other?

▶ What do they say to assistants?

▶ How are customers being approached?

Talking to customers in your own store is easy – you've got a badge on that says you are okay to talk to. Talking to customers elsewhere is a bit harder to do. Brits tend to be a little wary of strangers asking question but it can be done without you appearing to be a nutter. Most people do love to share their opinions, turn that to your advantage.

In your own store you can ask lots of open questions

▶ How well have we looked after you today?

▶ What do you think about how we've changed our displays?

▶ How easy was it to find what you were looking for?

▶ What do you think of these new products?

▶ How easy is it to shop in my store?

▶ What was the first thing you noticed when you came in today?

▶ What's your opinion on how I've set-up my till area?

▶ What am I missing in my store do you think?

▶ What sort of things do other shops like mine do that you really like?

When I'm in my civvies and out in somebody else's store, I find the most successful question tends to be 'I run a store like this one, what do you like about this shop?' and I'll be asking that usually while waiting in a queue at the tills. Lots of other opportunities to open up a conversation usually present themselves while wandering around the store too.

If the customer starts to chat happily, be conversational don't try to sound like a survey. People tend to respond along the lines of 'Oh I like the way they do X but I really wish they would sort out that damn Y'. Maybe we just like complaining but I have found over and over again that these little chats can uncover a glaring problem for you to look out for in your own store. Of course some customers will also happily give you a run down of what it is that attracts them to the particular store you are in and that's extra useful.

Turning the things we see into things we do

All of the above is just data gathering unless we do it with a purpose. That purpose is to find one thing to change in our own store today. I use a form like the one in Table.1.1. Everything I learn from a store, mine or otherwise, goes into the table. Then I prioritize each idea.

All of these you would consider doing

▶ Lots of benefit, easy to do, no cost.

▶ Useful benefit, easy to do, no cost.

▶ Lots of benefit, bit of effort required, some cost.

▶ Useful benefit, bit of effort required, some cost.

These you would not do

▶ Some benefit, easy to do, lots of cost.

▶ Little benefit, hard to do, lots of cost.

Coming back for more

Keep these tables and look back over them every quarter. Things might have changed in the store that make some of the borderline ideas worth doing now. It is also a great source of ideas whenever you are going for a job interview or moving to a new store.

Table 1.1 Store visit

Store visited: Bensons	When: 7 August 2003		Time of day: Early evening		
	What's the idea?	**What's the benefit?**	**Can we do it easily?**	**What's the cost?**	**What's our first step?**
Store	Their tie display is in a better place than ours is. Customers can linger over theirs longer and I saw people really taking their time before choosing a tie.	Moving our display out of the doorway and into a better spot might increase sales on that fixture. It's worth a try.	Yes. The display is portable and we can make room on the back wall easily.	Two hours of overtime one evening.	Find a volunteer for the overtime.
	The package promotion they are running on shirts bought with suits was generating lots of attention. Could we do the something better?	We can wow customers with a similar or better deal. We can also improve sell-through on some of the slower shirt lines.	Very easily, just need some POS and to feature it in our flyer. Might be worth doing an e-mail message to our data base too.	Discount on the shirt. Printed POS, although I think we can do a nice job with colour PC output slotted into a good picture frame.	Offer Gary the chance to pull this one together.
People	Bensons have got a really good suggestion scheme running. They have saved money from some of the staff ideas and earned money from other ones.	We can gather lots of good ideas if we have one too. These ideas could save us money and help us to sell more.	We'll need to create a written process for it but that's not too hard. Then it's a case of telling the team about it and then keeping keeping the profile up.	Mostly time cost. Like Benson's do, I'll pay staff a reward for each idea we use too.	Ask Jennie and Kevin to read up on idea programmes and then come back to me with a plan at Friday's team meeting.
Customers	A customer told me that they like the fashion tips that Bensons put up in the changing rooms. We can do that too really easily.	Adds value to the customer experience.	Very easy, we can put up magazine reproductions supplied by some of our manufacturers. And I'll see if someone wants to be in charge of adding our own 'recommendat-ions' and comments to those.	None, except a tiny bit of time cost to find and put up the POS.	Rob is our fashion guru, I'll see if he would get a kick out of having his opinions more in customers' faces!

2

Naked passion makes us great

Retail is a job of many skills such as leadership, an eye for merchandise, team-building, accounting, service and design. All these can to a greater or lesser extent be learned from a book. If you are weak in one or two of these areas you can still usually get by. There is one human factor above all others that is, however, utterly essential. You cannot be a successful retailer without it. Indeed, many fantastic old stores have been ruined, devastated, when taken over by people who lack this particular attribute. Passion is what keeps you trying, keeps you looking for new ways to delight the customer and to beat your competition.

Passion is what keeps you trying, keeps you looking for new ways to delight the customer and to beat your competition.

Passion is what drives retail, without it everything else is just playing shops. Just going through the motions, selling-by-numbers. All of the finest retailers, at every level from shop floor to boardroom, have a burning passion for retail. Passion drives great retail and customers, as well as colleagues, love it. Passion is the magic ingredient that helps you to bring surprise, drama, great service, exciting product finds and customer delight into the store.

Customers leave a store run by a passionate team feeling like they want to come back. The team itself looks forward to coming into work, knowing that today might be the day to break some records, have some fun and create something great. You could be a cashier at Morrisons or the owner of a dozen Body Shop franchises, so long as you feel that passion then the retail world is your oyster.

Passion to make things better

Passion is not about sales it is about improvement. Mahendra Patel is one of the finest passionate retailers I've ever met. MP, as we all know him, worked most of his retail life as a store manager and then as a senior field manager. Before that MP was a teacher in Uganda. In 1973 MP and his family had to flee for their lives in the wake of Idi Amin's murderous purge of the Ugandan Asian population. Arriving in the UK with nothing had, as you would expect, a deep impact on Mahendra. Many people would sink. MP didn't – he started out all over again, this time as a sales assistant in a shop. After 25 years in the business and having gone through so much, I couldn't understand why the ultra laid-back Mahendra always refused the many offers of promotion into head office and out of the field. He could have been running the whole show I would often, exasperatedly, tell him. I'll admit that I began to question where exactly Mahendra's passion was.

Passion is not about sales it is about improvement.

Then over a meal one evening Mahendra told me: 'I am a teacher, I always was. My job is to make as many people as I possibly can feel that they can be better than they are now, that they can improve their lot. Life is about hope and I've been lucky enough to give some people that.'

I don't think I ever saw MP sell anything, but his stores and regions always performed better in his hands than they had ever done when run by anybody else. MP's passion was for improvement. Not to create teams of sales animals but to make things better. Better for colleagues and better for customers. That passion is what makes this retail business great.

Case study 2.1 How Sainsbury's benefit from Jamie Oliver's passion

Passion can lead to some incredible outcomes. Take a look at the Jamie Oliver story; love or hate the Essex gravy-maker he is undeniably passionate about cooking. It is a passion that has transformed TV cooking. Experience Oliver making a bacon sandwich, I defy anyone (veggies excepted) to witness the energized passionate performance and not be desperate for a bacon butty themselves afterward. Sainsbury's have featured Oliver as a brand figurehead for some time now. This looks like a wise choice given that the period of Oliver's involvement coincides with an upturn in fortunes for the UK's second-placed grocer. What Sainsbury's recognized was that Jamie Oliver's energizing passion could also easily be brought into the store in the form of inspirational idea posters, enthusiastic recommendations and attractive recipe cards that customers really do respond to.

The Sainsbury's team could benefit though from taking this relationship further still. Walk into Sainsbury's amazing, cathedral-like, administrative head office at Holborn and right at reception you'll see kitchens. You'll see food, creation, the drama and theatre of cooking. Why is this not recreated in Sainsbury's stores up and down the country? Why isn't Sainsbury's regularly home to the evocative smell of garlic cooking, the fresh citrus tang of lemons just squeezed, the comforting sound of crusty rolls cracking open to reveal sexy soft sumptuous sweet bread inside? Just the words are exciting so why isn't this happening? The accountants and space planners might tell you that there isn't room. That to allocate space to demonstrations would damage sales per square foot. Operations and marketing people might not be keen because they would struggle to control the in-store activity from London. That loss of perceived control makes marketers nervous.

But that's all just excuses. Move-out the fluffy toys for a few hours a week, set up and heavily promote cooking demonstrations, tell people, make a fuss. Work that huge monetary investment in our Jamie and have him teach some of Sainsbury's own staff how to showboat: how to cook up a storm. Sainsbury's could even run the courses in those lovely show kitchens at head office. Staff will love it; they will fall over themselves to be involved. Customers will love it too; it will surprise and excite them.

Such passionate theatrical cooking demonstrations help sell more stuff. If the Sainsbury's team needed proof I would suggest they go and witness what happens at a Home Depot on demo day. Better still I'd suggest they get the expense account warmed up and take a trip to California for a walk around one of the brilliant Sur La Table stores where the passionate theatre of cooking makes them a bustling, exciting and money-taking success story. Sur La Table even charge customers good money to attend some of their cookery master classes and they get big attendances.

Passion makes things happen, it energizes the store. Passion is a performance improving tool.

3

Rising above the crowd

So with all this bursting passion we have for retail, the next step is to create some action, to make some changes. Lets say you work for Woolworths, I'm not suggesting you have to or anything, Woolies is just a good example of a big multiple retailer. If you really did work for Woolworths you would be a single voice among 28,000 colleagues. If you are going to accelerate your career, or you just want to get good ideas heard, acted upon and producing benefits for the whole business, then you have to raise your profile in the company. You have to become the one in 28,000 who everybody notices.

Raising your profile

Let's assume you don't work for one of the few UK retailers who have an effective ideas programme in place. Can you believe that so few retailers recognize how essential these programmes are? This means you will have to work a little harder to get your passionate ideas across. These are my top suggestions for raising your profile in a multiple environment.

If you are going to accelerate your career, you have to become the one in 28,000 who everybody notices.

Volunteer for things

Put your name forward for projects at all levels. You hear that your area manager wants someone to look after a roll out – stick your hand up for that one. Getting involved will bring you into contact with members of the central marketing team as well as senior operations people.

Such projects often turn out to be good fun, hard work but a nice break from the normal routine. The extra work also gives you a good opportunity to persuade your boss to strengthen your assistant manager positions.

Introduce yourself to people at every meeting

Go up to the MD at the next annual conference and say hello. Tell him or her who you are and where you work. If you have a useful point to make about the business or the presentations you have seen at the conference even better. Try not to corner them though, or you'll get a reputation for being a bit scary.

Make good use of the ideas programme if there is one

If there is a proper ideas programme in place, use it. Put clear sensible ideas into the programme whenever you can. Make each submission separately, that way you increase your chance of the evaluation committee noticing you.

Give people your mobile phone number

Whenever a senior person comes into your store engage them. Give them your mobile phone number and mention that you are always happy to have them bounce ideas off you. The best people at head office know the value of having people in the store they can turn to for 'reality checks' on ideas and projects.

Form an opinion

If you have something interesting and cohesive to say that will help you to appear more credible when you introduce yourself to senior people, don't be afraid to research and then rehearse that opinion. Both those things help to make you worth talking to.

Produce the goods

Success often does your talking for you. In whatever role you occupy make sure that you are delivering the very best possible performance. That's what this book is for, to give you lots of ways in which to meet and exceed your targets.

That's what this book is for, to give you lots of ways in which to meet and exceed your targets.

Specialise

Become an expert in a particular area, especially one in which you have previous experience. Read up on that subject, start to bring it into conversations, let people know that you are an information source and that you are happy to share your knowledge.

More thoughts on pitching ideas

Here are some issues you might want to consider when you prepare to pitch your ideas to your boss. Check that your idea is:

1 *Practical* – can we actually do this and can it be done using our existing resources?

2 *Affordable* – how much will it cost and from where can we raise budget for this?

3 *Supported* – is it likely that other departments, local networks or suppliers will happily support the idea?

4 *Customer focused* – put yourself in the customer's shoes: Is this going to make me feel good about your shop? Will I want to visit again because of this? Will it help improve my experience in your store? Will the savings you make lead to a poorer service for me?

Be a team player; ask your boss to put your idea on the agenda at the next team meeting. As you escalate the idea ask your line manager to make introductions. Offer to go and meet area managers, suppliers' reps and so on. If your manager tells you they would rather conduct the meetings themselves you have to respect that but you should also insist that you are at least present, if not talking, in the sessions.

It is important to retain ownership of your ideas because, either you and the team will get no credit when the idea goes live, or it just won't happen at all because nobody is really that behind it. Don't ever cut out your line manager though, that always embarrasses everyone. You might think your boss is a prat but it's their boss who hired them and who has backed them.

Be prepared for your ideas to sometimes receive a 'no'. It might happen a lot. Don't allow other to disparage you. Keep putting ideas and suggestions forward; you are raising your own and your team's profile in a very positive way. I guarantee that after a while you will begin to notice that your name gets put up for committees, area projects and so on. These special activities certainly make life more interesting but more than that; they give you and your team a chance to drive changes within the wider company. You become engines for positive change and that can be quite thrilling.

What if no one is listening?

If you try the steps above but find you receive nothing but rebuffs, then there is a chance that the doors are firmly closed for ideas. Maybe you even sense that senior management is wary of new ideas? If this is how it feels, not after one good idea gets shot down but after every good idea gets shot down you must vote with your feet. You must leave the company. Take your passion and potential to another retailer. I asked Julian Richer, chairman of the champion idea scheme users Richer Sounds, what advice he had for someone whose good ideas are being ignored 'come and work for us' was his reply!

I made a mistake, back in the early days, of quitting a good job with a big retailer because I thought everyone around me just didn't understand. I told myself that they were too stubborn to listen. It was years later that I realized that actually it was my impatience that was the fault. Be thoroughly honest with yourself before committing to a course of action that you could regret.

The truth is there are plenty of retailers out there who wouldn't know a good idea if you smacked them in the chops with it.

So consult people, people you trust. Get other opinions and perspectives but don't get sucked into a griping session. The truth is there are plenty of retailers out there who wouldn't know a good idea if you smacked them in the chops with it. If you are working for one of those you're better off out anyway. Ideas are the food for organizations, make sure yours are given a fair hearing; one of them might just make all the difference to the company's success.

PART TWO – **PEOPLE**

Make me happy and I will make you money

Picture: Koworld

4

How to build a great store culture

The best performance improvement strategy I could ever recommend to you is 'make your team happy'. A happy team of friendly motivated people, pulling together, having fun with customers, bristling with ideas and enthusiasm, people with passion for the job, can build huge performance improvements. Like so much in retail the recommendation to create a happy team is so very, very, obvious but is also a massive challenge. The best of us still struggle to get every new hire right. To always make the best decision in a given situation. To not drop the ball when the going gets tough. Management is hard to do right, that is why business rates good managers as assets.

Managing people is hard, great teams are the exception not the rule.

Because managing people is hard, great teams are the exception not the rule. That's actually a good thing for you. Think about it; if most retail teams are not bonding to aid performance then working hard to create a great team in your store will put you ahead of all those other stores where the team is not so strong. Think of it as competitive advantage through team building.

Building a strong team is one of the cornerstones of a great store culture. A great culture might sound a bit grandiose but that is exactly what you are striving to create. Creating a strong, positive and productive culture is something that has to come from the heart, how you do it is a reflection of who you are. That said there are four consistent cornerstones supporting all great store-cultures:

▶ *Cornerstone*   *1:* a clearly defined *mission* – what are we here for?

▶ *Cornerstone*   *2: respect* for each other – treat others as we like to be treated.

▶ *Cornerstone*   *3: recognition* of contribution – saying 'thank you' properly.

▶ *Cornerstone*   *4:* positive *team* building* – building a team that is good together.

*Leadership is important too but I believe great leaders and great team builders tend to be the same people

I'll go into each cornerstone in more detail over the next few pages but first I want to illustrate the value and importance of a great store culture. I would also like to show you that your individual store culture can still be a great one even if the wider company culture isn't.

The benefits of a great store culture

Cost savings

▶ Reduced shrinkage – happy people don't steal from you and they care more about reducing customer theft as well.

▶ Reduced employee turnover – happy people stay with you longer and that means savings not only on advertising for replacements but also savings on training and your time.

Improved customer service

Customers prefer to be served by happy friendly people, every observational study proves that conclusively. Tied in to the improvements in employee retention are corresponding improvements in employee effectiveness and knowledge. People who stay with you longer tend to get better at their jobs and that filters through directly to the customer experience.

Walking the talk

We cover values and mission statements later (don't yawn, were talking practical advice not management consultant waffle) when I'll explain why these are so important to the success of your business. A great store culture makes an excellent starting point for making values and mission statements really work for you. Walking the talk also means that new ideas tend to be adopted more readily and more happily by the team, everybody is up for driving the team forwards.

Support

You could create a happy team by letting everyone run riot, throw sickies whenever they wanted and help themselves to whatever they fancied from the stock room. That of course wouldn't do anything for the performance of the business. A great store culture still encompasses the unpleasant things such as sacking people who don't make the grade, and reprimanding staff when they let the team down. However, if you have got that great culture built and you have a happy team, they will tend to be far more supportive of you in those difficult decisions. That's useful because it helps keep the disruption of such moments down to a minimum and the team gets over it more quickly.

Enjoyment

Happy teams are nicer to work with. Fun is a powerful component in a high performing team. In all but a few circumstances, customers like getting to go out and buy stuff, so it's reasonable to aim for a fun store culture too.

Reasons not to?

A lot of managers say 'the company culture is so awful that I can't make a difference here in my store'. While I'm sympathetic to the additional pressure a bad company culture puts on its store managers, I can't accept this as a real excuse to avoid building a great store culture. Retail superstar Julian Richer has this to say about the ability of a store manager to lead culture in their own store 'the culture of the store is determined by the manager and then we try to get our company culture on top of that', (2001). It's managers who create the store culture not head office.

Why assistant managers must become 'keepers' of the culture

Richer also remarked that 'it is sad whenever a store manager leaves.' It is indeed sad when a great store manager leaves and it can often mean the death of a team. This is why store managers should work closely with their assistant managers in planning and building a great culture. Aim to leave a little bit of yourself behind so that whoever takes over, ideally your ASM, can strengthen the culture further, building on your work. For most of us, and I include myself in this, there is massive pleasure to be had from discovering that something you helped build is still solid and in play years later.

Case study 4.1 C&A – gone but with pride intact

You can create a great store culture under adverse conditions. When C&A UK's Dutch parent company decided to shut down the UK operation they called in a number of motivation consultants. The C&A business had been present on the UK high street for decades, so closure was quite a shock. The consultants were asked to look at measures to help preserve employee moral during the long wind-down period. This was because C&A were keen to keep as many employees on board till the end.

C&A were tied-in to many of their leases, so it made sense in those locations to continue to trade from the shop until the lease was sold on. The stores were closing, everybody was losing their jobs, many had been with the company for more than ten years, some for twenty or longer. A very sad time as you would expect, with the risk that many employees would decide to quit early to get on with their lives elsewhere, leaving the stores to operate with just a few staff.

In the end none of the consultants were needed. What happened was revealing if not entirely a shock. Against a terrible backdrop employee morale actually rose; teams pulled together with a blitz spirit, aggressive clear out pricing pulled in the customers, those customers regained their goodwill for the store and a fun kind of controlled mayhem reigned. I also picked up a sense that the store teams wanted to prove the parent company wrong by producing big numbers. Indeed many did record their best sales figures in years, albeit at a much-reduced margin. What this extreme story proves is that teams, operating in adverse conditions, can still create strong positive cultures.

Cornerstone one: the mission

Practical people slaving away at the coalface have a rational dislike of mission statements. We tend to think of them as nothing more than marketing waffle. I suspect that is because we have been subjected to so many awful mission statements that just didn't mean anything. That's a shame because a good mission statement is an incredibly powerful tool. It becomes a rallying point for the whole team.

Has your company got a mission statement? If it has, does it make sense? Does it make clear what it is that the business wants you to do? Above all, does it help you to make choices and decisions? If the answer to those questions is 'no' then you are going to need to re-write the mission statement yourself. Once you have done that you must make that statement live and breathe; refer to it in every team meeting and offer up every decision and choice you make against it.

Picture: Koworld

This is a store that knows exactly what it is for

Parcel delivery company TNT and Britain during the expansionist reign of Elizabeth the First (oh honestly!), provide two of my favourite examples of mission statements in action. TNT had a mission statement that read 'To deliver every parcel on-time'. Is that blindingly obvious? Yes! What this simple but powerful mission statement did was to focus every member of the business on the company's purpose. 'Will spending millions on our new software update help us to deliver every parcel on time?' If the answer is 'yes' then you get on with the analysis, but if it is 'no' then you have just saved the company a costly mistake. It always makes me laugh when firms invest millions in things that any bloke off the street could tell them will not support the purpose of the business. Incidentally this mission was later replaced with 'service is our only product.' What the hell does that mean? Have they given up delivering parcels, I'm confused?

A strong, clear mission statement can be a fantastic tool for improving and securing best performance.

My other favourite is the original mission statement, the one that built the first British Empire. Today we might feel a little uncomfortable about aspects of the British naval domination that enabled this tiny country to claim vast swathes of the planet for its own. What is undeniable though is that this was an extraordinary achievement.

British warships sailed the world under a very simple mission statement: 'for the Queen's greater good'. In any given situation British commanders could ask themselves 'If I sink that ship, or make a garrison, or secure this island will it be for the Queen's greater good?' If it was, then they would do it. Simple, clear and effective.

A strong, clear mission statement can be a fantastic tool for improving and securing best performance. Make it is simple, obvious, reinforcing and make sure too that it addresses practical objectives. Incidentally while writing this book I've had a mission statement pinned to the wall next to my PC monitor. It says 'To show retailers how to secure long-term success from happy teams and happy customers'.

Values

This is another area where a lot of awful rubbish has been spouted by management gurus. It means that talking about values can feel a little ridiculous. This is a shame because a set of defined values becomes the practical tool that helps you to apply the mission statement to the everyday running of the store. Where the mission statement tells you what the company does, the values tell you how it wants to go about doing it. They are a reflection of what the company stands for. We're talking about a list of words such as; innovative, fun, honest and inspirational. The trick is to mould these values into a set of practical sentences that tell us how to apply the values to the jobs we do every day.

A good way to test a set of values is to give them to someone outside of the company and ask them to describe what sort of workplace they think those values describe. If what they tell you accurately reflects what you want your culture to be then there is a good chance that you have got the values right.

Case study 4.2 Words we can live by

Tescos have one of the best defined mission statements and supporting set of values in retail. They are clear, easy to understand and they are relevant. Tescos have consistently applied the same mission and values throughout its surge forward in British grocery retail. The company now enjoys the number-one position in the market place having sat behind Sainsbury's for decades. That is a massive achievement, one which visionary former chairman Lord MacLaurin and the current chief executive, the brilliant merchant Sir Terry Leahy, put down to the Tescos team; all 140,000 of them.

Here is that superb Tescos mission statement (they call it a core purpose but that means the same thing as far as I'm concerned) and its supporting values in full:

Mission statement

'To create value for our customers, to earn their lifetime loyalty.'

Values

We do this by embracing the following values:

▶ No one tries harder for customers.
▶ Understand customers better than anyone.
▶ Be energetic, be innovative and be first for customers.
▶ Use our strengths to deliver unbeatable value to our customers.
▶ Look after our people so they can look after our customers.

Treat people how we like to be treated:

▶ There's only one team . . . the Tesco Team.
▶ Trust and respect each other.
▶ Strive to do our very best.
▶ Give support to each other and praise more than criticise.
▶ Ask more than tell, and share knowledge so that it can be used.
▶ Enjoy work, celebrate success and learn from experience.

See how they have split the values into those that relate directly to the customer and then those that relate to the team. That's an unusual but useful split. From experience I can tell you that it makes defining your values easier to do. Consider making the same distinction as you build your own set of values.

Walking the talk

Defining a good mission statement and then living the values in store 'walking the talk' is good for you because it improves the customer experience and builds stronger teams; which in turn increases business performance. In a case such as the Tescos one walking the talk in store is doubly powerful because everything the central team does, such as advertising, promotions and store investment, is also right in-line with the mission and values. They strengthen each other.

If you work in a business that has a clear and consistent set of values use them to your advantage. Live and breathe them 'walk the talk' it will improve performance. In an independent store you too must define a mission and a set of values, everything else flows from them.

Doing it for yourself

Unfortunately, most of you will be working in an environment where there is no defined set of values or a mission statement. Worse, some of you will have a set but they will be awful, some terrible product of a couple of expensive meetings between the HR director and a consultant. Neither of whom have been near a real store in years. You will know if your mission and values fall into this second category because nobody, not even the really clever kid who only works on Saturdays, will have a clue what you are supposed to do with it.

A good mission and set of values reads like the Tescos one, in language that a normal person can easily make sense of. In my experience there are only a handful of retailers who do have a clear, well-communicated and helpful set of values that everyone works to. There are others but some of the best in the UK include Tescos, Pizza Hut, Richer Sounds, Starbucks and Asda.

I had the pleasure of meeting with one of the top people at one of our largest retailers recently. On his office wall was a poster proudly talking about the company's new mission statement and new set of values. I asked him how the roll-out was going. He said 'The board are behind it, and people here at head office are living the values.'

'How about the stores?' I asked.

To his credit the director gave an honest answer 'Not so good there, we've not really cracked it in-store yet so the teams aren't working to the mission statement or the values.'

I had to hide a wry smile as I remembered sitting in the same building three years earlier listening to the same story. Of course three years ago they were talking about a different mission statement and a different set of values. Now they had changed them because they hadn't worked. They won't work this time either. I don't believe it is a coincidence that this particular firm has been in the doldrums for years now, it doesn't know who it is so how can its staff or for that matter its customers know either?

If anyone I've had a meeting with recently thinks this is you, here is how I would solve your problem. I would invite ten colleagues in from the stores and let them tell us what the values should be. I would allow them to re-write the mission too if they felt it was wrong. I would ask them to think about how to usefully apply their set of values to the business. I guarantee this would ensure a better result, one that the whole team, not just head office, could trust and buy into.

Case study 4.3 Values in action at a leading fashion store

Here is a solid practical example of the way in which values can make a significant difference to the everyday functioning of your shop. This case study is about a British clothes retailer. One of the very obvious values that applied to this business was that buying or selling clothes was about fun; it's a fun thing to do. Customers wanted a happy environment and staff wanted to enjoy their jobs. In fact that was one of the things people told us had attracted them to the business; working in fashion retail looked like it might be more fun than stacking shelves. So we included fun as a value. It really supported the company mission too. That mission statement read 'To delight our customers by giving them affordable access to great high street fashion.'

Fun is a value that many people believe, and I agree, should be part of the working environment for almost any retailer. I don't mean mindless larking about but the generation of genuine 'this is cool' moments for customers and staff alike. Fun helps make shopping enjoyable. We are all in the business of making shopping fun, whether we are selling washing machines or watches.

Fun with job descriptions

One of my favourite methods for making values work every day in store is to re-write job descriptions. Out goes the dry HR-speak and in comes practical stuff about what to do and why. In the case of this retailer we had identified one particular group of employees who were really hard to engage. There was a set of 16–18-year-old girls who all worked one week day evening and then all day Saturday. They are notoriously hard to engage. You hardly see them all week then suddenly they are there on your busiest day when you've got little time to give them. It's crucial that you have these girls on board and pulling for the team or they can become a disruptive and negative element in the store. They are also famous for micky-taking degrees of lateness and for being uncommitted when they do finally arrive. This was especially true on hung-over Saturday mornings!

We looked at their job descriptions which, and to be honest I can't blame them, I doubt any of the girls themselves had read them. One of the most important responsibilities, in fact the first task they were supposed to perform on Saturday mornings, read like this: 'You will ensure all merchandise rails, shelves and/or islands are fully filled and merchandised in accordance with the prevailing marketing planogram for your store grade and profile.' Of course what this actually meant was simply 'Make sure there are no gaps on display when we let the punters in.' The girls regarded this responsibility as a real chore . . . boring. Not the sort of thing they wanted to do when arriving tired after a big Friday night out.

So we changed it, we introduced that value of fun. The same line from the job description now read 'Fashion is fun, remember that as you dive into the stockroom and pull out your favourite, most exciting fashions. We want you to take your choices, the clothes you think customers should be wearing out tonight, onto the sales-floor. Get them onto the racks, anywhere there are gaps, and get your choices noticed.' When we trialed it the effect was fantastic.

Because we had asked the girls to think for themselves – and who really is best placed to say what the trendiest clothes for 16–18-year-old girls are than a group of 16–18 year old girls – they actually got excited by the task, even beginning to come in early to get the best picks. They also got competitive with each other and would jostle for space and monitor each other's selections like hawks. Very healthy stuff indeed with the unexpected side effect that the girls also began to sell proactively. They would make sure every customer saw their personal picks and they would ensure a constant supply of sizes and colours was always out on display. That's how a mission statement and a clear set of values can have a direct effect on the performance of the team.

Cornerstone two: respect

The mobile phone retail business enjoyed, or suffered, a yo-yo sales curve during the 1990s and into the 2000s. Even excellent businesses such as Carphone Warehouse and the best independents were not immune when the market first dipped sharply. But when picture messaging and colour-screen phones sent the mobile phone market back upwards, these retailers benefited more than most. Carphone Warehouse is the honest phone retailer that emerged out of a time when the sector was dominated by sharks and cowboys. This is a retailer that prides itself on looking after everybody's needs, customers and staff alike. It is a retailer whose success-ful employment policy is built on respect. It is also a retailer who has ben-efited from the very positive knock-on effects of such a policy.

Talk to an employee of Carphone Warehouse and they will tell you that the work is hard, the hours long and that the standards are stretching and rig-orously applied. They will also tell you that they enjoy it enormously. Push a little harder, ask them 'Why do you enjoy it here?' A consistent story emerges:

→ We get treated with respect.

→ I'm trained so well that I never look stupid in front of customers.

→ My ideas are worth something.

→ I'm allowed, no I'm encouraged, to use my brain.

→ It's made clear that I can have a proper career at Carphone Warehouse if I want one.

Carphone Warehouse were one of the leading beneficiaries of the 2002 upswing in mobile sales. Before that most-recent upturn a saturated market place had pushed down prices and margins. Unit sales volumes had been significantly down too. These were tough conditions for survival and indeed some didn't survive. Not even award winners such as DX Communications could pull through the doldrums. Forgotten them? Exactly. Their presti-gious award, incidentally, was a sales growth award. And grow they did. Too much capital invested, too many stores and not enough attention to the individual shops, customers and employees.

By 2003 the bad times appeared to have gone and the future looked bright again for mobile phone retailers. Carphone Warehouse had weathered the storm because they had looked after customers and employees. The respect they show to staff shows in the respect staff show to customers. As a result, the majority of customers stayed with the Carphone Warehouse business through the bad times even though they knew they could buy the same phone cheaper elsewhere.

An alternative approach can be seen in the same marketplace. In 2003 Phones 4U featured in a fascinating TV documentary. In one now infamous scene a manager was shown enjoying the dubious honour of receiving what could be considered as quietly threatening phone calls from his millionaire chairman John Caudwell. These phone calls were to remind that manager that he had but one week to improve the numbers or face the sack. That's a classic example of management by fear rather than management by respect. I asked Phones 4U how they felt about the picture portrayed in that documentary. They told me the result had been an upsurge in job applications from people they called 'real go-getters, the sort of people who respond to a bit of pressure'. I'm interested to see how this will pan-out for customers over the long term.

The failure of fear

Management by fear has a name, we call it: JFDI, or 'just flipping do it' (you and I both know that I've changed one of those words to a print-friendly alternative). I hate these techniques but here's the sting, so too do customers. They notice. They might not be able to define what it is that they notice but it does affect them. They can feel the negativity in store and can experience it through the service they receive. Mobile phone retail offers a brilliant lesson in why JFDI is a terrible way in which to run a retail business. The pattern in this market sector proves that the technique doesn't work long term, it shows that it is unsustainable.

In a fast-growing market, where price and availability are the overriding considerations, many customers will happily buy from the cheapest outfit regardless of reputation. The situation then changes quickly when the market conditions tighten and saturation is reached. In the slowdown customers gravitate to quality, they think a little more carefully about what they want and they look for reliable sources of good advice. Then, when things begin to pick-up again customers often stick with the new relationships they've formed. They value those relationships with retailers who have looked after them knowledgeably, honestly and with a smile.

It is those retailers who have built-up a mutual respect between themselves and their employees who are more likely to provide customers with that knowledgeable, honest and friendly service. Retailers such as Carphone Warehouse are even able to command a premium because of the strength of reputation they have built over the years. Customers are willing to pay a little more to receive a great reliable service.

This effect is just one very good reason to train, recognize and respect your staff. Forget even the straightforward cost benefits of keeping your staff longer, the simple reality is that teams built on respect and passion ultimately bring more profit into your business. Teams built on fear and unreasonable pressure do often create short-term sales gains but they always crack, and usually this happens very quickly. What is more they leave customers feeling negative about their interaction with the company and less inclined to ever come back again. In an age when head office, area managers and you too have real-time access to the day's sales numbers it can be easy to fall back, under pressure, into a JFDI management style. Don't. What your business gains today it will lose tomorrow and next week.

> **Teams built on fear and unreasonable pressure do often create short-term sales gains but they always crack, and usually this happens very quickly.**

The respect deal

Respect, thankfully, is a two-way street. Yes you will still have to deal with under-performing colleagues. Yes you might find yourself having to exit people from your business. That is always hard to do but in a team that has been built on respect you will have worked hard with that person to make things right. The people in your team will know that and will support your decisions rather than become unsettled by them.

We have that phrase 'You have to earn respect', well in retail management that gets warped a little. You, as a manager, have to earn respect from your team sure, but you must respect them from day one! People are always wary of change, which is why you will have to work hard to earn their respect. But this is not a mutual deal. Even before you first meet your team you have to respect them. If you don't, if you come into a new store with an attitude that said 'I'm in charge and until I know you I am reserving my judgement' then people tend to turn off.

Earning and at the same time giving respect means swallowing your pride sometimes but things are that way for a reason. Brits tend to be a naturally cynical lot and we don't like working for a new boss. We distrust them by instinct. Work studies prove this. What this means is that your team start their relationship with you assuming that you are going to be incompetent, unfair, heartless and temporary! But if you start off in the manager role, assuming the same of your team, they will either quit or make your life unbearable.

Luckily, the most effective way to earn respect is to give it! If you systematically go about building trust, recognizing people's contribution, sharing training and creating opportunities for personal growth then you will build a strong successful team that likes and respects you. You will have gone a long way to building a brilliant culture.

For some great tips on how to build respect read Chapter 5 which is on Motivation, I've listed a whole series of them there.

Case study 4.4 Benefits of risk

A major supermarket chain decided to allow all of their thousands of employees, at all levels, to authorize customer refunds and mark-downs. Can you imagine the security director's panic 'Do you realise how exposed to fraud that makes us?' That director's job is to be worried, to assume everyone is out to rob the firm. You can always tell which office is theirs at head office: the door is closed and locked, the lights cold and bright and the eyes of the occupant always a bit shifty. Can you imagine how scary it must have been for him to have to risk-plan a scenario where cashiers at twenty tills, fifteen hours a day, 365 days a year over hundreds of branches could theoretically be making markdowns on every single transaction they process? It is the stuff of absolute nightmares.

What actually happened is remarkable and it is a brilliant illustration of how giving employees their self-respect back can inspire improved performance. Yes, some staff did use the new system to rip-off the supermarket. They would put through bogus refunds for their mates and would markdown items in their Mum's shopping every week. But the majority of staff didn't do that. In fact they got such a kick out of being trusted in this way that they began to police the activity of their colleagues themselves. It became very hard to be fraudulent because colleagues would report the fraudsters. The majority felt so pleased that the company trusted them they wanted to keep hold of the privilege. They recognized that to do this they needed to stop cheating colleagues from ruining the system.

The net effect was actually a decrease in employee-related shrinkage because staff generally became more aware of employee-related theft. Shrinkage as you know comes right out of profit not revenue so every percentage point reduction in shrinkage is of massive benefit. Customers too liked the effect this new rule had on their experience of shopping at the store. No quibbles, no waiting for the supervisor, just a straightforward 'Oh that's on its sell-by date today, would you like to exchange it or shall I put it through at half-price?' A very motivating win-win that came as a result of this company having a respect for the integrity of its team.

Ownership – the value of mistakes

People make mistakes when you let them make decisions. They get a lot right too. Being as close as they are to where the action is your team are absolutely the best people to be making more decisions for the business.

Durning the 2003 National Retail Federation New York conference I went to see George Whalin, arguably America's best independent retail mind. Before we sat down for a chat I watched George deliver his conference address. George has a lot to say about helping independent stores to stand out and this was the subject of his seminar that day, a Sunday incidentally as if emphasising just how hard we retailers work.

What appeals especially to me about George's philosophy of nimble retailers adding value and creating customer delight, is that it is practical, real, proven and repeatable. It is scalable too; what works in one store will work in 100. Because it is scalable it was no surprise to discover that a number of senior people from the big chains were dotted around the large audience. I knew this because I'd earlier enjoyed a comic game of surreptitious delegate name badge reading.

I spoke to a number of the directors and senior managers. A common theme emerged, they seemed to be there almost despite themselves. It was as if these people wanted to hear George speak just so they could then dismiss his thoughts as 'fine for the independent but not realistic across my chain'. I asked them 'do you think George's ideas work?' and they all answered along the lines of this typical response, 'Yes, and he's got the numbers to prove it.' I went on to ask them why then could these ideas not work in their chain? A director of Petsmart gave a typical reply 'our problem would be managing all this additional promotional activity across our various channels and stores'. No it isn't! That's your opportunity. Give your managers the scope to make things happen for themselves. Create local-promotion kits, train managers, give them budgets and a little freedom, and then let them go for it.

It is easy to see how senior central management can get scared about letting their store managers loose. But all the evidence tells us that this is wrong. Wherever proper decision-making power has been delegated down to individual store teams it has led to increased sales and profit. Yes it has also, sometimes, resulted in more mistakes being made. But mistakes are only unlearned lessons. You make one, you learn from it and you move on. Maybe that sounds a little too much like a homespun philosophy but it also happens to be true. Think about the early careers of people like Richard Branson, bankrupt in his teens, or Ray Krok the genius behind McDonalds who had a string of mistakes, false starts and lean times behind him when, at 62, he spotted the potential for franchised fast-food. Mistakes are made when you try something new, different or difficult. Sure you reduce your errors down to zero if you never try anything but just see what happens to your business when you do that.

Case study 4.5 Decision making at Timpson

One of Britain's most successful retailers is a brand that you may not be able to immediately recognize. Timpsons was a mighty shoe empire that hit hard times some time after it fell out of family ownership. The inspired merchant John Timpson fought for 15 years to buy back the family firm, only to sell it again just three years after winning that fight. The instinctive Timpson could see that tough times were ahead for shoe retail, so he sold out to the Olivers chain.

Timpson did however retain part of the business – the shoe repair and key-cutting outlets that had formed a tiny but profitable part of the Timpson group. Some years later the British Shoe Corporation collapsed despite at one time enjoying a 20 per cent market share, while Timpson repair shops traded very successfully. At the time John Timpson remarked: 'Some people realized it was a good decision to get out of footwear retail, no-one knew how smart it was to keep the shoe repairs.' He is entitled to that self-congratulation. The Timpson shops are fantastic examples of what can be achieved by encouraging store managers to think like owners.

Many of the instinctive tenets of what Timpson calls his 'Upside-down Management' philosophy are similar to those found at Richer Sounds and Asda but two stand out as unusual even among that pioneering group:

1   Managers are allowed to set their own prices if they feel the company price list is wrong for their area – this enables managers to deal very effectively with keen local competitors, to help promote the shop and to improve margins where possible.

2   Timpson pay staff £2 to fill-out customer complaint forms. The best businesses embrace complaints as a superb free learning tool but to pay staff for them is exceptional and brilliant.

I like the way John Timpson does business and I respect enormously that he still visits his shops every day collecting ideas, complaints and improvements. Timpsons offer a superb insight into what happens when managers are encouraged to make real decisions for themselves. It is no coincidence that, along with those other visionary retailers Asda and Richer Sounds, Timpson regularly appear in the top half-dozen places of the *Sunday Times'* annual 'Best Companies to Work For' awards.

Cornerstone three: recognition

→ My boss notices me.

→ Whenever I step-up my game people here say 'thanks'.

→ The atmosphere here is good because the company spot you when you are really walking the talk.

Whenever you walk into someone else's store ask a couple of the staff there this question: 'Is this a good place to work?' Whenever one of those people answers 'yes' push them a little further, ask them 'why?' If you hear any of the responses listed at the top of the page you will know that this is a team where recognition is contributing to a great culture.

Recognition is literally the habit of catching people doing good things and then saying 'thank you'. It is the single most powerful motivation tool business has ever been given. Motivated teams give better customer service, work happier together, are more efficient, are more stable and they make life at work more enjoyable for all. That is because when you recognize an employee's contribution you send out a very strong message that says 'I'm glad you came to work today, you made a difference.'

Most people want to do the best job they can in any given situation. Recognition is the tool that tells them it has been worth making the effort. Recognition is self-reinforcing, people want to do a good job, you recognize them for it when they do, they feel good so they repeat the recognized action because they like feeling good. This is a simplified representation of what actually happens but do you see how small moments of praise can escalate into improved performance?

Given that recognition is so powerful why is it that new store managers are almost never trained in, or assessed on, their ability to effectively recognize? I believe there are some simple reasons. The first is that recognition is hard to get right. Many of the moments that you will benefit from recognizing, saying thank you for, are hard to measure. They might include such things as improving team spirit, giving exceptional customer service, or going the extra mile. Recognition is less about direct sales numbers although you will want to recognize contribution in that area too.

I suspect that it's the free nature of recognition that puts number-obsessed chain retailers off using it. This is a trust issue, head office not being prepared to trust that fact that it is managers in the store, on the spot, who have the best view of the people around them. Recognition is free it doesn't cost a penny and can drive store performance more effectively than almost any other management tool I have ever seen. You simply must use it.

Please don't make a fuss

One of the issues that makes recognition hard to do at first is a cultural one. The British are embarrassed by praise, we struggle to accept it. Indeed the most common response among British workers to receiving praise is to blush and to break eye contact. The strange parallel to that praise response is that we generally do not have the same problem when receiving criticism. When on the receiving end of criticism most British workers will listen, not always graciously, but they will listen. We all tend to have a system for receiving criticism, maybe not always a positive system but it is nonetheless a system. When it comes to receiving praise, although we really like the feeling, we are a little unsure of how to react.

There is also a crucial difference between the British delivery of praise and of criticism. We tend to be specific when criticising but only general when praising. It is this lack of clarity I believe that makes Brits so bad at giving and receiving praise. We give specific criticism such as 'the budget you did isn't right, where are the print costs?' where praise would be vague; 'nice work on the budget'. This is important because the whole point of praise and recognition is that we do it in such a way that recipients understand exactly what they did well so that they can repeat that behaviour. In the budget example above the person who has been criticised knows they have to now go and sort out the print costs. The other person, praised with the 'nice work on the budget' comment has no idea why this budget was better than the last one, or what it was exactly that they ought to repeat to get some more praise next time. Better praise would have been 'I like how you've laid out the budget, that's going to make it easier for me to get it approved. Thanks.'

'Doing' recognition

'Little and often' is a brilliant management maxim. It's absolutely perfect when applied to recognition. To make too much of a moment of praise can make everybody feel uncomfortable. It can even sometimes encourage resentment from the team towards whoever you have singled out for extra-double helpings of praise. You are not attempting to make an individual feel like they are God's gift to retail. If the thing they've done is really special then by all means mention it at a team meeting. Spot something good, mention it quickly, say 'thank you', be specific.

The bad recognition habits we managers get into, often because we're embarrassed by praise, include: worrying about singling out individuals, delaying praise, over-blowing praise, concentrating on catching people getting it wrong and the inability to be specific with our praise. Delaying praise reduces the effectiveness of recognition. Recognition works best when fresh.

Too many people build their management style around spotting staff making mistakes and then correcting the errors. If you are one of them try catching people doing good things instead. Do that and you will quickly find that staff actively attempt to repeat those good things and that they look for more and more good things to do. Recognition taps into so many crucial psychological needs. The easy bit to accept is that recognition, done properly, makes people feel good.

It is nice also to link recognition sometimes to small rewards but this actually isn't at all critical. Study after study shows that the part employees actually value is that moment where their manager, or a colleague, or a customer, says 'thank you for . . .'

Behaviours

Although a good recognition habit is all about being spontaneous saying 'thank you' whenever you see the need, it helps to have in mind a list of the sorts of things that you will be looking out to give praise for. At the risk of sounding like I've been snacking on a jargon butty, what you should be basing your recognition on are 'observable positive behaviours'. Essentially that's all the good stuff people do that you can spot them doing.

When you first decide to introduce recognition, putting together a list of these 'observable positive behaviours' helps the whole team to get a handle on what it is that you are looking for. Once you've sat down and really thought about these behaviours you can stick a list up on the noticeboard. Give a copy to new starters, and use it as a basis for review meetings.

'Observable' is the key word in this bit of jargon. It tells you that the behaviours you are looking for are those that you actually have to 'see' happen. Sales in not an 'observable positive behaviour' because it is an activity that (a) you already measure closely in the performance numbers, and (b) you will be discussing the sales action with each member of the team anyway. What would be an 'observable positive behaviour' is when you spot someone going out of their way to make a customer happy. With any luck that behaviour will show up as a sale too, but even if it doesn't that customer has left the store with a good feeling about your business. That is worth its weight in gold but in a way that is very hard to see from looking just at the hard performance numbers.

Case study 4.6 Positive behaviours observed at NatWest

Before a recent trip I needed to get hold of some Canadian Dollars. I went to the small Marlow branch of NatWest. It was the nearest to me at the time and as a NatWest account holder I got commission-free currency exchange there. As usual I had left things till the last moment, I was flying the next morning and this would be my last chance to get the money before the airport.

The cashier told me that she 'didn't hold Canadian Dollars.' Very politely she added that she could order them in for tomorrow or she could phone the larger NatWest in Oxford and have some put aside for me. Good customer procedure but not at all helpful for me right then. I replied that I was flying tomorrow and that a trip to Oxford wasn't possible. Without a pause she said 'Oh, in that case I know that Thomas Cook on the High Street keep Canadian Dollars, try them instead.'

Now, think about that. I've not seen the training manual at NatWest but I have at a number of their rivals. I'm pretty sure it will not say anywhere 'If we have do not have the required currency then send the customer to Thomas Cook.' But why not? I did get my Dollars from a rival but I still felt great about the help I'd received from NatWest. As part of my on-going relationship with NatWest that cashier had delivered on the promise to give me the help I want to meet my financial needs.

That cashier's action is an 'observable positive behaviour'. Something you can't measure in the normal way but that is very effective in supporting the mission and in making the customer very happy. This is exactly the kind of behaviour that you would do well to single out for recognition.

Easy ways to 'do' recognition

There are two easy routes you can go down to build specific recognition into your team culture. Doing specific recognition needs to be learned so don't be embarrassed that it might not be part of your current style. You will get there by practise. Equally don't assume that because you do often say 'thank you' that you are getting recognition right. I'll lay down good money that, when you are honest with yourself, you will find that 90 per cent of those 'thank you' moments are non-specific.

Method one – the 20-second ceremony

Use a couple of team meetings to make up your team's list of 'observable positive behaviours'. A good way to get a great list together is to start with the company mission statement and values (if they exist) and think about the kind of things you can do to support them.

Now make up some 'thank you' notes. These should have space on them for the recipient's name and a bigger space for you to write down why you are pleased enough to want to say 'thank you'. Print out a bunch of these and keep some in your pocket at all times. Whenever you see an opportunity to say 'thank you' fill one out quickly and go put it into the hand of the person you want to say 'thanks' to. You don't even have to say 'thanks' if you don't feel you can. You don't have to make a song and dance of it, you don't even have to speak if you feel uncomfortable. What is important is that the exchange of this note is something both of you understand: it tells the recipient that you have noticed and that you are pleased, nothing more, nothing less.

Dish out blank 'thank you' notes to the team too. Encourage everyone to use these 'thank you' notes. Workmates recognizing each other's efforts has almost as much power as when you do it. You have really cracked it when you get customers to fill in 'thank you' notes too.

The 20-second ceremony works so well. It is unobtrusive too. I've seen this work successfully in a mad-busy tiny KFC that was processing 50,000 lunch transactions a week. People really do respond to it. The notes can feel a bit silly at first but that soon goes and the process of recognition becomes part of the every day team culture. You will never find a cheaper or more effective way in which to transform your team's performance.

Method two – the heroes board

Allocate a piece of wall space to recognition. Make-up some 'thank-you' notes similar to the ones mentioned above. Start giving them to people under the same criteria, and tell recipients to bang them up on the wall. This method introduces a little bit of peer pressure because everyone can see who is being praised, but you might find it more comfortable for you than recognition method one.

In both methods you can use the best examples to determine what you do with your non-cash rewards (which we go through in Chapter 5). It's quite nice to build in a little focus at team meetings for recognition. It's even more effective to use one such meeting, each week, for a little bit of extra recognition. Take the best 'thank you' or 'hero' example from that week and give the person a decent bottle of wine, a case of beer, flowers or good chocolates. Not too much but it feels great to receive and it really sets the scene for a rousing and effective team meeting.

Case study 4.7 KFC and the 20-second recognition ceremony

KFC transformed their business in the UK in the late 1990s and have strengthened their position ever since. It is a fantastic retail business. One of the major transformation focuses was on the way in which they treated their people. As part of that process they introduced a recognition programme based on observable positive behaviours and on the 20-second recognition ceremony.

A beautiful example of how this tiny, simple, ceremony could effect the way people felt about themselves and their performance came to me at a post-launch regional meeting. A manager, Mike, told me what had happened when he went through the 20-second ceremony for the first time. In fact he told me he'd made somebody cry doing it so I thought we might be in trouble. Dawn had worked at her KFC outlet for nearly 10 years. She had seen managers come and go but had never been keen to take on that sort of extra responsibility for herself. She liked being one of the team and that was that. Mike had been her manager for nearly six months.

One morning Mike spotted Dawn showing a new member of staff how to 'double bag' a waste bin. Double bagging means putting in two bin-liners at a time so that at lunch, when the bin is full, you only have to throw one bag of waste away and the bin already has its next liner in place. Now this is a tiny thing, saves maybe a minute at peak time. But Mike saw Dawn do this and it occurred to him that he had seen Dawn help new people learn the ropes on countless occasions. She didn't have to, it wasn't part of her job, she just liked to do it. So Mike decided to use one of his 'thank you' notes. He wrote it out and ticked a box that said 'For making new members of the team feel welcome' and, in his own words he 'shyly handed it to Dawn'.

Dawn burst into tears, Mike reassured her that it wasn't a P45 he'd just given her and asked what the matter was. So she told him 'You've never said "thank you" to me before.' Mike became quite indignant and replied that he had, often, at shift meetings. Dawn put him right 'No, you've said "thanks" to the team at those times, and that's nice but you've never come to me, looked me in the eye and made it so clear that something good I do has been noticed. And actually none of my managers over the years has either.'

Dawn felt great about that moment of recognition, that's why there were tears. So do most people. What's so nice about this approach is that its effect snowballs. Slowly but surely, more people begin to repeat the good things they do more often, and that gently spreads throughout the business.

Cornerstone four: team-building

There are no hard and fast rules for team-building, how you do it is very dependent on your character. Your judgement, a bit of luck, the existing tools you have available and your personality all contribute to what counts and what doesn't. Read a few books on the subject and you get to see some contradictory ideas, *The 1-Minute Manager* (Blanchard, 1983), for example, often contradicts Tom Peters (1989) on leadership, and Stormin' Norman Schwarzkopf suggests a whole load of team-building ideas that actually fill me with fear. If you are interested, the best book on team-building I have ever read is Sam Walton's *Made in America, My Story* (1992). This terrific read talks about how he and the team built Wal-Mart – the world's most successful company. Using easy, jargon-free, homely language and descriptions, he captures all the important rules of team-building. I've taken some of Sam's headings and used them here because they are so good. The descriptions though, are mine.

→ Communication

Share information, it builds trust.

→ Choosing the right people to work with

Work with people you like and people who broadly share your world view but who you think will still challenge you when necessary.

→ Credit where credit is due

If someone has done a good job, tell them and tell them right after they have done it. A timely thank you makes people feel like it was worth bothering to do something good.

→ Knowing when to quit

If it isn't working stop doing it and try something else, that way you get to try lots of things without bankrupting the team.

→ Delegation

People like to do responsible things, it makes them feel trusted and respected. Delegating good jobs, not just the stuff that you don't like doing, leaves you better able to get on with taking the team forward.

→ Letting people make choices

Most people at work want to do the best job they can, if only you'd let them! Allowing people to make their own decisions builds their self respect and they need to have plenty of that before they can begin to have respect for you and the team as a whole.

→ Listening

Shut up and listen to what people are telling you before you go making up your mind. Ask questions and allow people to give you the whole story. People respond better when they feel they are being listened to.

→ Making everybody responsible for each other and their own actions

At first sharing responsibility does lead some people to feel they have an opportunity to make mistakes and hide them. Before long though the team begins to see that sharing responsibility means that its actually okay to admit you got something wrong and then together fix that mistake for everyone's benefit.

→ Celebrate success

Absolutely essential to the strength of the team is making time, and plenty of it, to celebrate success. I don't mean the embarrassing forced stuff such as ringing a bell every time somebody makes a sale though. Celebrating success means saying 'well done' to people. It means making a small fuss of good things in the daily team meetings. It means going off for a pizza and a beer together. Toasting a hard-won target feels great. It feels even better if you've talked one of your suppliers into paying for the beer.

People need to know that the effort they've put into achieving something had a point to it. Celebrating success is one critical way in which you can do that. It says 'I'm proud of us, we took on a challenge and we beat it together'. I cannot stress enough that you will gain many times benefit from putting aside a proper budget for doing this.

→ Being able to admit your own mistakes

If you get it wrong be honest about it and move on, 'Okay I got this wrong, now how can you help me to do this right next time?'

→ Respect and trust

We've gone through a whole section on respect so if you haven't read that one yet take a look now. Respect and trust are the absolute critical bonds of team building.

→ Strong values

Values reflect the culture. They also create the framework for you to build your team upon.

→ Putting the customer at the centre

The customer is at the centre of all this action. It is the customer that we really work for. They are the ones who pay our wages. Teams need to have focus and in retail the customer is the best target for that focus. Everything you do must be built around the notion of helping customers to leave the store with a smile on their face.

More headings ...

To Sam's list I'd like to add these that I and others have recommended over the years. These are quite specific to retail and you are forgiven if they make you giggle with recognition!

→ Square pegs do not fit into round holes

Some managers appear to get a kick out of juggling their people, 'stretching them', putting an employee into a role outside of that person's experience, ambitions or interest. It rarely has a positive effect.

→ Don't let your star salesperson get away with being lazy

If your best salesperson is annoying colleagues by creating a trail of mess, paperwork and customer service issues then they are probably annoying your customers too. These people sell lots but they put customers off coming back to you.

These people find it very hard to change their habits, often they just can't. It is tempting to put up with the disruption for the sake of the sales they bring in but ultimately these stars are a liability. You will have to consider letting them go.

→ Boat rockers, no matter how intelligent or creative they are, are bad for teams

These are the individuals who become frustrated by rules they feel unable to respect. They want to change things but they have no patience. They always undermine the management team. See if you can find a way to ship such people out to head office where they do more good than harm. Special projects are a good home for them and for the ideas they do sometimes produce.

→ Don't bad mouth people

Every time you say 'so and so is an idiot' in front of your team you send a negative message about your attitude to colleagues. Negative talk infects your team, just don't do it!

5

How to get people out of bed

Motivated staff are critical to the success of your store. Hopefully you will have already read the previous chapter on store cultures. If you have, then you are already on the way to enjoying the benefits of having a motivated team around you. In this section we're going to get right to the nitty gritty of motivation. In particular I'd like to suggest some practical moves you can make to improve the motivation of your team.

If you're going to build a great culture in your store a motivated team is essential. Just to recap, the benefits of a great store culture include cost savings, customer service quality improvements, people pulling together to deliver the company values, better support for your decisions and a more enjoyable time at work.

The components of motivation

Individuals are motivated by a combination of:

➜ Financial reward

➜ Implied sanction

➜ Self-respect

➜ Non-financial reward

➜ Recognition of value contributed.

Of course the impact of each motivating component will be different for different people. Factors such as age, personal circumstances and social considerations all have an impact. Most of these make for only really subtle changes in your approach though, with one exception. The younger members of your team are often disproportionately motivated by cash.

Financial reward Show me the money

The most common mistake we all make on motivation is to assume that financial rewards are the most important and most motivating thing we can offer. The truth is – and this might be hard to accept because it is counter-intuitive – that money has very little motivating effect beyond a certain point. So long as the wage is fair anything over that such as special bonuses or massive cash competitions has very little additional impact on employee motivation. It can even be counter productive because the payment of large bonuses tends to condition staff to only ever put in extra effort if they can see a wad of cash in it for themselves. Pay too little however and money becomes an astonishingly important demotivator.

Those retailers with the most motivated workforces have observed that offering significant cash rewards in exchange for performance improvements has three effects:

1 It drives too much focus into short-term revenue generation at the cost of falls in customer service quality.

2 It conditions employees to only go beyond the job description when they are offered a cash incentive to do so.

3 Bonuses become absorbed quickly into the employee's general budgets and as such are not remembered over the longer term.

There is a whole filing cabinet full of research that suggests that cash triggers only very short-term satisfaction in the mind of the recipient. It boils down to cash being, by its nature, ephemeral – here today and gone tomorrow. I know you probably still don't believe me but this effect has been observed time and time again. Money is important but it doesn't create long-term motivation. You might need to trust me on this one?

Incidentally you can measure employee motivation by looking at factors such as employee satisfaction, employee turnover rates and customer service quality scores.

Implied sanction | The stick to your carrot

Implied sanction is the stick to your reward-carrot. It is the rulebook. It's 'implied' because you may never have to use it but the team knows you would if pressed. It's 'sanction' because it's what happens when the list of minimum standards is not met. Implied sanction is a strong motivating factor but one that requires significant skill to manage effectively. It takes a lot of common sense too, and certainly sympathy with the concept of 'treat others how you would like them to treat you'.

A sales assistant, for example, needs to know that a drop in customer satisfaction will lead to a serious chat. Further they must know that the serious chat will generate a set of actions that, if not carried out, will cast serious doubt over their future in the store. That's the sanction part.

The team needs to know that sanction is possible but at the same time they must not be working in paralyzed fear of that sanction. It's a tricky balancing act sometimes but much better than the alternative which is to manage by fear. Management by fear generates lots of problems such as a decrease in service quality. Frightened staff don't work well with customers. Fear can also lead to increased employee turnover and even industrial disputes.

In the 1980s hard-bastard macho managers dominated retail management. Fear was a powerful motivator then because unemployment hung over pretty much everyone all of the time. Times have changed. There have been retail vacancies going unfilled in the UK for some years now. Management by fear is a poor technique but we must recognize that we're all human. A lack of sanction for those times when we let standards slip lets us become lazy. To motivate you must ensure that the team knows you have set standards for a good reason and that you will maintain them vigorously.

Successful one-to-ones

When you have to actually use sanctions be quick, be clear and be fair. Here's the best format for a one-to-one in which you have to discipline a member of your team.

➜ 10-minutes to explain the general principles of the situation.

→ 5-minutes to very specifically discuss the weakness or failure of the individual.

→ 15-minutes to then explain why you have faith in that person's ability to turn around the situation. This is time to re-build that person's belief in themselves and their abilities. Make sure you finish the meeting with the person feeling on a high.

You can probably see a lot of the *1-Minute Manager* in that process and that's fine. This is the practical way for retailers to do the same thing. Over the years a number of store managers have recommended variations on this method to me, but I'd like to specifically credit Umesh Vadodaria of PC World for this version.

Self-respect | Treat me like a grown up

The default position for the majority of British workers is to do the best job we can. If you create the right conditions most people will work hard to deliver a good result. What stands behind that reality is self-respect. I've already talked about how the best teams are built on respect, and self-respect is a crucial component of that. It's what makes people feel like its worth making the effort.

If you create the right conditions most people will work hard to deliver a good result.

The opposite is also true: put individuals into situations where they are robbed of their self-respect then they will react accordingly. People will steal and treat customers with contempt and why not? If you take away somebody's self-respect how can you ever expect that person, in turn, to respect your customers?

Without wishing to get horribly political I'd like to ask you to take a look at what poverty and unemployment do to communities. Take away a person's job, put them in a cheap house they don't own or ever could then crime, drugs and malcontent flourish. The truth is that if I don't respect myself I'm not going to respect you. You can do such a lot as a store manager to encourage self-respect to grow among the members of your team.

Share information

Tell the team the confidential stuff: state of the cash flow, company health, costs, losses and profits. Show that you trust them with such sensitive numbers. Yes some of it will find its way to your competitors but the losses will be vastly outweighed by the benefits.

Delegate power

Allow team members to make decisions for themselves, especially on discounts and customer service issues. Give people the confidence to make these decisions by ensuring that you have a good set of practical and sensible guidelines in place. Good procedures help people to make good decisions.

Encourage training

Make sure everyone who wants it has access to all of the training opportunities available. Make a habit of promoting manufacturer-sponsored training and seminars too. These are often of a high quality and they make a welcome break from the usual company formats. You are saying to the team members who go on these courses 'I value you and I want to give you access to skills you'll find useful.'

Share the good jobs

Make members of the team responsible for specific tasks, especially those 'cushy' jobs managers sometimes keep for themselves.

Muck in

If you expect the team to polish and dust; do it yourself too, show that it is not a job that's 'beneath you'.

Listen to both sides

When a customer complains listen to both sides of the issue. Don't blame the sales person in front of the customer; you are responsible for service quality so you make the apology. Then go talk with the sales person and if there really is an issue give them an opportunity to suggest ways in which to solve it.

Don't wash your dirty linen in public (even if you run a dry cleaners)

Never embarrass or dress-down a colleague in public. I once observed some bully of a manager having a go at a cleaner in front of customers. This cleaner had been skiving but that didn't matter, the manager ended-up looking like a nasty piece of work. That reflected badly on the shop.

Delegate responsibility

Make members of the team responsible for the performance of specific departments. Responsibility is a powerful source of self-respect especially when combined with a variable such as profitability or sales revenue.

Consider the rule book

Is there anything really daft in the rule book that just forces people to do stupid things? If there is then get rid of it.

Let others do the talking

Give everybody who wants to a chance to run team meetings. Encourage staff to present ideas at these meetings too. Go with the three slide rule to prevent meetings becoming too competitive or boring: One to set-up the 'what it is', one to explain the 'how it is' and a final slide to summarise 'why it is'.

Encourage every opportunity for feedback

Get and give feedback on ideas, interviews, worries, suggestions and concerns. Do this in an honest active way. Take things on board. If the answer to an idea or issue is 'yes' then get on and do it. If the answer is 'don't know' go find out what you need to know. If the answer is 'no' explain why. Offering a shrug and a 'because it just is' is never acceptable. Always do these things within a short timeframe.

Build people back up

If you have ever have to pull somebody up, discipline them or criticise their performance then always build that person back up again afterwards. Leave people on a high.

Recognition

Learn to give specific praise as well as specific criticism. This is really very hard to do at first but is the most powerful motivating force of them all. Recognition is free and makes a real difference. By giving recognition you are giving person X a reason to feel that 'getting out of bed and coming to work today was worth it'. The key to recognition is to be specific, to do it as soon as you think about it, and to do it little and often.

Using non-financial rewards Lets have a laugh now

'Non-financial rewards' is just a name for the fun stuff. They can include all sorts of things such as extra days off, flash cars for a month, gift-vouchers, freebies and holidays. Now there is a really fine line here between exciting and tacky. It's so easy to make rewards embarrassing. Worse, lots of retailers go for the big dramatic holiday type incentives where only one person can win anything significant. Maybe the best performing store manager gets to go to Bermuda for a fortnight. I've often worked with clients, employing thousands of people, who have insisted on running these demotivating incentive structures. They launch huge incentive programmes worth big money but concentrated into maybe five prizes only. Fantastic for the lucky five but actually all this succeeds in doing is turning off the thousands who are pretty sure they won't win. Worse out of the 200 who think they are in with a chance 195 high-achievers are left feeling positively demotivated when they don't win that holiday.

When it comes to all motivating rewards, including cash bonuses, recognition and non-cash bonuses, little and often is best. In this case 'little' because that means you can spread the budget much further and in doing so touch far more people. 'Often' because it keeps things fresh and gives you lots of opportunities to boost performance without programmes going stale.

When it comes to motivating rewards, including cash bonuses, recognition, and non-cash bonuses, little and often is best.

It's how you use the little non-financial rewards that's critical. As either an owner of an independent or as a chain-store manager you have lots of freedom to do

Picture: Koworld

Shopping is fun, we should all remember that

what you think will work best. Buddy up with the manufacturer's reps. Let them do some training at your store one evening and suggest they give the expense account a workout by taking the team for a curry afterwards. I'm always pleasantly pleased by how consistent manufacturer's reps are in this regard. They always say 'yes' eventually.

As an owner of a store you should be doing these things anyway, out of your own pocket. Incidentally, building in an ideas session before you eat is a good way of recouping the cost.

The wrong way to use non-cash rewards is to over-hype the reward or to use inappropriate rewards. So, for example, offering to give someone a CD for doing 200 per cent of their target is an insult to you both. Wrong too would be to make a shy person stand on a chair to receive a commemorative 'Top Guy' plaque. Use your best judgement and knowledge of the individual – what works for one might well turn off another.

Buy the team a daft gift each at Christmas but hand-write a thank-you note on each package. It reminds people that they are important to you. Always generously mark people's birthdays, weddings and new babies. Preferably do so out of your own pocket rather than via a staff whip round.

Try to include your employee's partners on social invites. Partners have a massive influence on your people and on their view of you. A career in retail features strange and challenging hours that take people away from their families. Don't make that worse by extending this exclusion to the team's social occasions. Getting partners involved in idea generation can be very effective too.

Great non-cash incentives produced out of almost nothing

A good tip is to save any freebies you receive as a manager and pass them on to the team rather than keep them for yourself. Some managers save up these goodies and freebies to use in one go. Others dish them out straight away. Either way you must ensure that you don't fall into either of these traps:

1   Only ever giving stuff to the loudest members of the team because they are the ones you notice.

2   Showing favouritism to a person whom the team could, conceivably, suspect you of having more than a professional interest in.

Here's two ways of avoiding these freebie pitfalls and at the same time bringing some fun to the proceedings.

Team ballot

Say you've been lucky enough to find yourself with four bottles of champagne, two boxes of Belgian chocolates and a stack of good promotional T-shirts. It happens! Over a week you have the team agree to nominate a colleague each for a thank-you. All they have to do is write down the other person's name and a line on why they should be thanked. The key to participation is that anyone who doesn't make a nomination is disqualified from winning a prize themselves.

Then you all pile down the pub after close-of-play one evening. Get a round in then read out the 'thank-you' notes. Everyone who has been nominated gets to choose a random envelope. Try to make sure everyone who should have been has been nominated. Inside each envelope is a note telling them which of the freebies they've earned.

This is effective because the team sees that you could have held onto all the stuff yourself but preferred them to have it, people love that, they really do. Asking them to self-select worthy recipients gets people focused on their place in the team too. Team ballots are not heavy affairs but they really do work, aim to run one every six months or every quarter at a push.

Balloon day

This method of giving away all your freebies can be hilarious, great fun, nicely competitive and very motivating. On one of your busiest days you fill your office with balloons. Each balloon contains confetti and a little envelope that has the name of a prize in it. To spice things up a little, I usually chuck in some envelopes with 'fivers' in them and some with a token for something silly like a choccy bar in them. Then you draw up a big chart with the names of all your team on it.

Now you need to set a challenge. Challenges can include such things as:

► To sell a specific item.

► Gain an 'excellent' score on a customer service questionnaire (do this as an exit survey, have someone stand on the door with a clipboard gathering answers).

► Selling add-ons, score a point for every transaction that includes a legitimate add-on (legitimate meaning the add-on was actually something that the customer will have been glad to have been sold).

Each time a person completes a unit of the challenge they earn a 'pop'.

You can also award random 'free pops' to members of the team, especially to anyone who isn't actively involved in selling. Do this whenever you observe a positive behaviour. Those positive behaviours could include such things as solving a customer complaint or helping out a colleague. Each time a person earns a 'pop' they get a token. These tokens are sticky and you can encourage people to stick them on the poster as the day goes on.

At the end of the day, after the punters have gone home, everyone gathers outside your office. Maybe you open some refreshments to help get the team revved up for the popping to commence. Starting with the person who has earned most 'pops' you let each person into the room to pop the number of balloons they've earned during the day. Then they get to keep whatever falls out of the balloons.

I've run this one many times and it always gets everybody going. It's nice too if you can make the balloon day coincide with a team night out afterwards too. There are lots of variations on this theme such as having the prizes in lockers or in a sandbox and so on. I'm sure you can think up some yourselves too.

Recognition and motivation

Each of the motivating factors we've gone through here does in itself also have a recognition component. Giving out prizes is recognition, trusting somebody to make decisions is recognition and bonuses are also a form of recognition.

6

All we need is a little better every time

Ideas are the fuel for organizations. What you do with those ideas, how you convert them into action and improvements, is what makes the organization grow and prosper. Space for improvement can be readily found in all areas, especially in technique, systems, presentation, recruitment and performance. All retailers can benefit from a culture of everyday performance improvement but few try to. Don Taylor and Jeanne Smalling-Archer, authors of the very helpful *Up Against the Wal-Marts* (1994) call this kaizen, as does Julian Richer in his awesome book *The Richer Way* (2001). Others use different names for the same thing. Kaizen is Japanese for 'continuous improvement involving everyone.'

I don't think we need to slap a Japanese jargon word on to the making of improvements. For me the task is as simple, and as vital, as 'lets do it a little better every time'. That sets up a very simple question for your team members: 'How could I do this again only better?' Your mission statement comes in here because it helps define what 'better' means. At TNT whose mission used to be 'to deliver every parcel on time' 'better' would mean: faster, safer or cheaper. For retailers 'better' will usually mean; faster, cheaper but still better for the customer.

Improvement in this sense isn't necessarily about massive earth-shattering changes. What we are looking for are those every day improvements. Improvements in the ways in which we look after each other, our relationships with customers and the quality and relevance of our processes. A typical example might be the discovery that one piece of paperwork can be integrated with some other process rather than dealt with separately. Combining the two will save money and time, so that's an improvement. It could be the realization that the rules of a promotion we've created can be simplified to the benefit of the customer, and that is an improvement too.

Gathering improvement ideas

You will need to have two things in place

1 A way to gather ideas.

2 An improvements slot on the agenda for discussion at team meetings.

If you were to look at just one task or process in each daily team meeting you would have seven improvements each week, 30 for the month and 365 over a year. That's awesome. Okay, so maybe you won't get into this every day but you will still generate a significant store of improvement ideas every month. Working in this way is easy. You are not attempting to change the world in a day, you are just looking to change one little thing at a time. Every journey starts with just a single step, remember that.

> **If you were to look at just one task or process in each daily team meeting you would have seven improvements each week, 30 for the month and 365 over a year.**

Do you currently change anything each month? Does change only ever happen dramatically once a year? 'Lets do it a little better every time' puts you in the driving seat of change. Your team becomes a valuable engine of change.

Statisticians are blind – the measurement trap

Plenty of otherwise sensible people believe that you cannot improve that which cannot be measured. That's dangerous, wrong even, and here's why: some of the most effective customer satisfaction-improving tools are un-measurable in a conventional sense. Smiling at a customer – warm genuine smiles not the fixed leer of the street nutter – has proved to be one of the most effective ways to make customers feel better about you and your company. How do you measure the number of smiles your team gives out?

Here's something to think about: a number of aspects of sexual performance can be measured. Factors such as duration, the dimensions of various body parts, room temperature, heartbeats/minute can all be easily recorded and measured (you might need somebody with a clipboard to come in and write this stuff down for you though). But do any of these factors automatically add up to guaranteed great sex? Of course not.

Measuring the wrong things is a real trap. This is a grim example but its worth telling: a US Army General noticed that the daily success of the Vietnam War was being measured by relative casualty rates. A measure as crude and unpleasant as 'if we kill more of them than they do of us then we must be winning'. Convinced that this measure did not convey a useful picture, the General instead created a set of metrics that also took into account territory, specific objectives and economic cost.

It is what the General said about his reasons for doing this that is absolutely relevant to retailing. He said 'we are only making important that which we can easily measure when actually we should be measuring only that which is important'. Just because you can measure unit sales easily for example, does not make that the most important part of your business to concentrate your improvement efforts in. Customer satisfaction is harder to measure but far more important because it relates to unit sales made today, tomorrow and next year.

Go with your gut feel

Use your gut feel and allow yourself to apply improvements even to those processes, tasks and interactions to which you are unable to attach numbers. I'd like to ask you to consider valuing the power of your gut feel more highly. Gut feel isn't random. It's a guide, an instinct that tells you a certain path may be the right one to take. It is also that good sense which tells you not to do something. But it needs tuning, books like this one exist to help you separate out correct gut feel judgements from other emotional factors such as fear or laziness.

> **Even science is now beginning to come round to seeing gut feel as something real and valuable.**

Even science is now beginning to come round to seeing gut feel as something real and valuable. There is a credible theory that suggests decisions made on gut feel are more often than not the carefully calculated result of our experience and knowledge and that instinctive gut feel decisions get better as we add new experiences and knowledge to our memories. Think of your gut feel as a potent business weapon, a weapon that is unique to you.

Making improvement work for you

Let's do it a little better every time. As well as running through ideas to apply this idea to at team meetings you will need to create an environment in which the team feels comfortable to try things, and to suggest things. If you are the kind of person who greets every new idea with 'I'd love to change that but . . .' or 'I can't see that working' then soon people will stop trying and suggesting. Equally if members of the team feel that you are likely to discipline them for making mistakes then no one is going to want to try anything new for fear of punishment.

Get the culture of improvement established. Allow your people to question how they do things and you will benefit enormously. Make that an everyday occurrence, little steps but lots of them, and you and your customers will feel those improvements take hold.

Where to look

The best retailers do not stand still when successful. They strive to keep the momentum, to keep growing and to keep moving forward. That growth and movement is inspired by tiny little everyday improvements just as much as it is by sweeping change.

Here are some of the categories in which you will always be able to find lots of opportunities to improve things. The thoughts listed here are a deliberate mix of actual ideas and of pointers to get you looking in the right places for ideas of your own.

You might like to pick-out a single line during daily team meetings and have the team come up with some thoughts and ideas on that theme.

Improvement and customers

▶ Consider everything from the customer's perspective.

▶ Encourage customers to tell you their complaints.

▶ Listen to them sincerely when they do.

▶ Think about the type of people who come into your shop.

▶ Make changes that bring people to you who currently shop at your competitors.

▶ Talk to customers all the time.

▶ Aim to improve average transaction values.

▶ Use eye contact.

▶ Walk your store like a customer would.

▶ If you can get hold of former customers ask them why they don't love you anymore.

▶ Whenever you are resolving a customer complaint ask customers how they would improve your service.

▶ Remember names.

▶ Think carefully about the integrity of your pricing.

▶ Send them stuff they might actually like to see.

▶ Where can you add value to the customer experience?

▶ What can you promise today that is better than yesterday?

▶ Run surveys.

▶ List the benefits of doing business with you and then tell customers about these benefits.

▶ What do other people do well that you really ought to be ripping off for yourselves?

▶ List all the things in your store that regularly delight customers – then think about how to double the list.

▶ Are you leading by example?

▶ Write down a list of all the processes that touch customers directly – all of them.

▶ Then do a list of all those that don't – can you strip any of these out?

▶ Make it easy for customers to give feedback to you – use suggestion boxes, till receipt surveys, telephone aftercare calls, open evenings and everything else you can think of.

▶ Get customer opinion on new products before you put those products into your range.

▶ Ask customers to tell you 'what's missing?'

▶ Ask customers to tell you what they like about your store.

Improvement and you

▶ Read stuff.

▶ Get involved in the business community – join your street or shopping centre advisory committee or the chamber of commerce.

▶ Ask people about your management style.

▶ Learn from those below you as well as above you.

▶ Seek out examples of great retailers and learn from them.

▶ Sign-up to every Internet resource you can find – here's three corkers for a start off: www.theretailbulletin.com, www.nrf.com and www.georgewhalin.com

▶ What things do you do outside of work that might be useful inside?

▶ Make an honest list of your strengths.

▶ Then one of your weaknesses.

▶ Go on courses.

▶ Sign up to every training and seminar resource you can initially – the more you go on the better you will become at recognizing which ones are going to be truly useful in future.

▶ As naff as it might seem, set life goals and then yearly goals for yourself – what do these goals tell you about the areas in which you will need to concentrate personal improvements?

▶ Listen to people more than talk to people.

▶ Open your eyes!

▶ Go shopping more often – do things your customers do.

▶ Read the trade press.

▶ Learn from competitors.

▶ Learn from people outside your sector.

▶ Maintain your standards.

▶ Appoint an honest and strong assistant manager – they will soon let you know where you have room for improvement.

▶ Improve the balance of your life, you look after shops – shopping is fun, try to see it more that way.

Improvement and colleagues

▶ Reward people for improving things.

▶ Consider issues from your team's perspective.

▶ Don't get mad with people for trying.

▶ Let grown-ups think for themselves – empower people to make their own improvements.

▶ Encourage talk, talk and more talk – leave every feedback channel open all the time.

▶ Give people a look at these lists.

▶ Recognize people's contributions.

▶ Don't rip off your staff.

▶ Never criticise employees in front of anyone else.

▶ Build a great culture founded on trust and respect.

▶ Tell people you are chuffed with them whenever they make you feel that way.

▶ Are your job descriptions a jargon-filled sack of nonsense?

▶ Feel free to build friendships but never forget that you are the boss – keep a perspective.

▶ Encourage the team to be open with mistakes.

▶ Have a laugh together.

▶ Always, always celebrate success.

▶ Be human in your relationships – if someone is going through a life crisis help them cope with it.

▶ Share the numbers – let the team own them as much as you do.

▶ Pay a profit-related bonus.

▶ Pay a customer-service-related bonus.

▶ Smile when you walk through the door every morning even if you don't feel like it.

▶ Make sure everyone knows about all available courses and seminars.

▶ Put aside cash for training.

▶ Let good people go on courses you've been on – use training as a reward.

▶ Be specific with instructions.

▶ Sales assistants get closest to your customers – listen to what they tell you about those customers.

▶ Challenge people and encourage them to challenge themselves.

▶ Teach by example.

▶ Show people that the best way to do things is to consider solutions rather than dwell on problems.

▶ Get the team involved in all the big decisions.

▶ Help employees to see that it is customers, not you who pay their wages.

▶ Hold regular one-to-one appraisals but be prepared to allow employees to tell you what they think of you, of your business and of the team too.

▶ Have a team meeting every single day. Just 15 minutes worth but make those minutes count (see Appendix A).

Improvement and costs

▶ Take a firm and consistent line on employee theft – always sack proven thieves and prosecute wherever possible.

▶ Walk the fine line between minimising customer theft and creating an unappealing high-security atmosphere.

▶ Prosecute shoplifters.

▶ Anything the customer doesn't see only ever needs to be functional and cost effective.

▶ Try to get stuff done right first time – especially the solving of customer complaints.

▶ Negotiate everything.

▶ Pool resources with other local retailers.

▶ Swap cost saving ideas with your neighbours.

▶ Keep track of all supplier rebates and discounts.

▶ Get more than one quote!

▶ Use e-mail for as many of your communications as possible so long as doing so does not make you look cheap to the customer.

▶ When prioritizing areas to look into for savings concentrate first on your largest cost categories – a small success in one of those can be worth much more than a big success in a tiny cost category.

▶ Check any special group rates negotiated by your trade association.

▶ Listen to what customers tell you they think is important – anything they don't rate highly is probably not worth spending so much cash on.

▶ Cut out the middleman wherever you can.

▶ New design-graduates are a much better and more cost effective option for your advertising and direct marketing than an ad agency is.

▶ When placing print orders, or booking a TV or radio advert always demand the agency discount – this is a 10 to 20 per cent discount that printers, radio stations and telly channels give to agencies, just because you book direct doesn't mean you shouldn't get the discount too.

▶ Make good use of government employment programmes but listen to your conscience – if it looks like slave labour it probably is slave labour.

▶ If an employee isn't pulling their weight and you have tried hard to help them you have to let that person go.

▶ Do any members of the team have any skills that might mean you can avoid hiring-in a tradesman? Pay the employee a proper bonus for any above and beyond jobs that they do.

▶ Measure where your customers are coming in from – improve or cut any activity that is not driving traffic.

▶ If you pay employees a profit related bonus then that will in itself help limit some of the unnecessary expenditure – so long as you are also sharing the store profit and loss information.

▶ Use your ideas programme to harvest all the cost saving ideas the team can come up with.

▶ Consider sharing savings with the employee who identified them.

▶ Be nice to suppliers and let them pay for stuff if they want to.

▶ Get rid of the waste – any process that does nothing for customers, or for you, just has to go.

▶ Look at these processes all the time.

▶ Re-use things whenever you can.

▶ Teach employees how to promote the business when they are outside of work.

▶ Renegotiate all contract renewals – insurance premiums especially can be slashed at these times.

▶ Ask the team if they know a way to get hold of something cheaper – years ago when we bought a horribly expensive colour photocopier it wasn't until the behemoth was delivered that one of the warehouse lads said 'New copier? I could have got you a discount, my Dad is regional director for Canon'.

PART THREE – **CUSTOMER**

Make me happy and I will give you my money

Picture: Koworld

7

How to make more money

There is no secret to performance improvement. The techniques can all be learned. But just as some racing drivers can make an identical piece of metal move consistently faster than that of a team mate, so it is that some retailers are able to improve performance better than anyone else. I've known a few racing drivers over the years and the best of them have one thing in common: consistency of line. They take the right line through more corners more times than anyone else. That's it, nothing magic or secret or unknowable. The same thing holds true when it comes to performance improvement. There is no secret. It's about getting the details right and paying attention to the fundamentals.

The rules of performance improvement are so simple that they can be understood instantly, and there are only four of them.

To improve performance

1   Sell to new customers.

2   Sell more in each transaction.

3   Persuade existing customers to return to your store more often.

4   Improve margin by cutting overheads and improving sales quality.

This is another of those 'it's not rocket science' moments. The challenge is of course in understanding how best to apply each rule. The chapters in this part of *Smart Retail* deal with those things you can do to produce direct results from applying these rules to your customers. People and store issues also have a part to play in the successful application of these rules but it is what you can do directly for the customer that has the most significant impact.

This part covers

1 Great customer service.

2 Sources of competitive advantage.

3 Promotions that work.

4 Real marketing for real retailers.

5 Package deals to close sales.

Priorities

If I was forced to choose just one of the four rules of performance improvement over all others, the one I would pick is number two 'Sell more in each single transaction.' Driving up average transaction values is all about maximising every opportunity. That in itself is a powerful business improvement philosophy. 'Make the very best of every customer who walks in' is your first consideration.

'Make the very best of every customer who walks in' is your first consideration.

Great customer service

First and foremost I'd like to dispel one important myth about customer service and competitive advantage. Great customer service does not provide any firm with a competitive advantage. Rather, great customer service is actually a pre-requisite for survival within, or entry into, any retail market. You must offer great customer service or you will not stay in business for very long.

When I first sat down and planned out *Smart Retail* I assumed that I should be writing a separate chapter on customer service quality. Service quality is one of the critical factors in the success of a retail business. As I talked my way around the world's best retailers it became clear that service quality cannot be 'taught' as a stand alone subject. It is at the very heart of everything you do.

Picture: Koworld

Great customer service makes people feel good about your store

Every decision you make must be in the context of 'will this be good for our customers'. Every person you hire must be someone you think customers will enjoy being served by and every process, promotion and event you choose must be for the benefit and delight of customers. Great customer service is not a bolt-on activity it is the only activity. As such every word in this book is written in the context of great customer service.

If service is poor, business will suffer. Customers have less patience for poor service than ever before and Britons have even learned how to complain. If there *is* one secret to great customer service it is the knowledge that great customer service begins with your people.

The roots of great customer service

Employee satisfaction

The most effective way to improve service quality is to improve the satisfaction of your team. Having a reward and bonus programme based around customer satisfaction scores can be really effective too. It helps your team to make a direct link between how they look after customers and what goes into their own pockets.

Feedback

Making it easy for customers to feedback to you is critical in improving service quality. If you haven't got a customer complaint process, one that's easy for customers to use, create one. Give customers quality surveys that they can fill in and send back to you. Give them pre-paid envelopes to make it even easier for them to do that. Give out your e-mail address and your telephone number. Encourage complaints and think of them as free market research. Some customers will rant and rage but at the heart of almost every complaint is a truth that, once learned, will help you to make your business better.

Some customers will rant and rage but at the heart of almost every complaint is a truth that will help you to make your business better.

And finally it is better that customers complain to you, and that you resolve their complaints, than it is for them to complain about you to their friends instead.

Case study 7.1 Great service makes the difference for Boots

If a woman in Oxford wants to buy Clinique products she has three stores to choose from. She can visit Debenhams, Boots or Allders. These stores are all within two streets of each other. Clinique is a high-margin product and therefore important to the performance of the beauty counters in those stores. It is more expensive than many other make-up brands too, so strong sales in Clinique will contribute to the raising of average transaction values.

So then how to choose which shop to buy Clinique from? Prices, across all three stores, are identical. The display systems and ranges in each are identical too. What changes is the staff on the counters. It is they who can make an absolute difference.

Janet buys all her Clinique products from Boots in Oxford. She does this because Beverly on the counter there offers outstanding customer service. Beverly knows her product, is friendly, approachable, and crucially she has a phenomenal memory for names, faces and skin-types! She greets Janet by name each time Janet visits. Often Beverly spots Janet walking in the store and makes a point of approaching and saying 'Hi Janet, how are you?' and then giving Janet a free product tester. Sometimes, quite often in fact, this results in a sale-on-the-spot but Beverly doesn't push for that and is never disappointed when no money passes hands.

Janet trusts Beverly, whose specialist knowledge, friendly manner and likeable personality make her a fantastic sales person. That's the direct benefit of exceptional service.

8

Where competitive advantage comes from

Most management books will give you a definition of competitive advantage that goes something like this: 'Condition which enables a company to operate in a more efficient or otherwise higher-quality manner than the companies it competes with, and which results in benefits accruing to that company.' That's fine for a textbook but for us out here in the real world a more useful definition of competitive advantage might be: 'that fleeting moment when we have done something that is more attractive to customers than our competitors have.'

Areas in which you can achieve competitive advantage

There are various areas in which you can achieve competitive advantage but really it's about mixing a number of techniques in a way that consistently 'wows' customers. One of my favourite retail exhortations is that we should delight the customer. If you keep that in mind whenever searching for a competitive advantage then you will do okay. 'Customer delight' in itself provides moments of competitive advantage.

> **One of my favourite retail exhortations is that we should delight the customer.**

These are the main areas in which you might look for competitive advantage.

Specific promotions

Individual offers and events that beat the competition. I've set aside for you a whole chapter later on choosing and running great promotions. Make sure you read the thoughts on price competition before skipping off to that one though.

Promotion types

Taking leadership in a particular type of promotion. Boots have done this using two-for-one and three-for-two price offers. These offers are built right into the Boots business model. Indeed most Boots suppliers have to agree to fund a number of these promotions during every promotional period. Many customers visit Boots just to check out the two-for-one promotions.

Product niche specialism

A very effective option for smaller retailers who can build a deep range within a single product sector. A specialist reputation can help attract people to your store. Customers learn that you offer a better choice and better advice in this one area. Manufacturers are often quite keen to support this activity too.

A specialist reputation takes a little longer to establish than one for say bargain pricing. That specialist reputation though will last for years, sometimes even lasting beyond your tenure at the store.

Case study 8.1 Specialism at Tony Hillam's

For twenty years Tony Hillam ran a hardware store located just outside Cleckheaton in Yorkshire. Tony retired a few years back but still, purely for the fun of it, works holiday relief in the store he sold. That is retail passion in a nutshell and should tell you a lot about the type of retailer Tony is.

The Cleckheaton store, which still bears the name Tony Hillam, has two complementary specialist reputations. In the winter Tony Hillams is the best place to buy your Calor Gas but it is the summer specialism that works so well for the store. In summer customers travel miles, sometime fifty or more, to talk lawnmowers with the Hillam team. Tony stocks an extensive range of models, parts and accessories. On most lines Hillam's matches the equivalent B&Q price and on some he beats them. Crucially though the store's reputation allows it to stock additional high-margin specialist models that would be slow movers in one of the big DIY sheds.

It is not just the choice and range that attracts customers, it is also the ready supply of friendly and trustworthy advice that is always on offer in the store. Truth is we English love a mower and can't help wanting a lawn beast that is better than our neighbours' machine. Tony Hillam's specialism helps create a pleasant place in which its customers can indulge that little garden pleasure. An environment that makes the buying, running and maintaining of these machines a treat.

Added value

You can add value to the customers' experience in a range of areas. Activities that add value include such things as:

- ▶ Product demonstrations.
- ▶ Masterclass technique demonstrations
- ▶ Product training for customers
- ▶ Tip sheets
- ▶ After-sales service
- ▶ Trade-in
- ▶ Expert staff
- ▶ Credit facilities
- ▶ Loan product availability
- ▶ Pre-order facilities
- ▶ Bespoke services such as tailoring
- ▶ Specialist product ordering
- ▶ Delivery services
- ▶ Free samples

▶ Try-before-you-buy

▶ Convenience

▶ Design services.

An added value experience is somehow more than just a list of extra services, its an attitude – part product of the culture, part conjured by the store environment, all added to a mix of competitive techniques.

Case study 8.2 Expert added-value inside a chain-store

Expert staff can create powerful added-value in a chain store environment. If you have a member of the team who is passionate and knowledgeable about a particular product category consider putting them in charge of it.

Here's a simple example of how you might do that. If you sell movies and you have an employee who is expert in this area who loves films and is friendly and good with customers then let that person promote the movies section of the store. Challenge them to select films for special focus promotions. Have that person write-up some review cards to attach to shelf edges and encourage them to talk to customers about selections.

I remember finding such a person running the audio-visual section of WHSmiths in Oxford some years ago. His enthusiasm lit-up that whole area of the store. He talked to customers, asked them for their opinions, made recommendations based on what they told him and pointed out offers that he thought might appeal. On one occasion I watched this department for fifteen minutes. In that time this informed, friendly, passionate chap sold two extra DVDs and a copy of a promotional VHS to customers who had not appeared to have considered these additional items until he had highlighted them. All three customers appeared delighted with these discoveries.

The enthusiastic assistant had generated an additional £45.97 in those extra sales and in doing so had increased his average transaction value. I think he served six or seven customers while I observed. I left the store with a lot of respect for that chap, as I imagine his customers did too. If I had been recruiting in Oxford I would have tried to poach him. Do you have someone like that in the team? They could create an added-value competitive advantage for you if you have.

Price-led positioning

More and more retailers are opting to take up price-led competitive positions. They have chosen to occupy a specific predictable pricing band. Incidentally, over the last decade the value price proposition has been the most successful price-positioning in world retail. There are a number of different price-propositions as well as the value one. Modern supermarkets offer an interesting insight into these categories where a single store might feature sections catering to one of perhaps four different price propositions. Tescos, for example, offer their plain-label discount brand, competitively priced branded products, added-value delicatessen counters and then handpicked speciality treats where price is almost not an issue.

Price-led positions

1   *Value* – good quality merchandise at a predictably low price, that would include New Look, Wal-Mart, Aldi, Poundstretcher and George at ASDA

2   *Added value* – mix of value pricing and some premium pricing but added to such strong added-value elements that customers feel it is worth the premium. Stores such as Londis would feature here where their added-value is convenience. Carphone Warehouse are another example where honest reliable advice is part of their added-value.

3   *Beyond value* – store where price is simply not an issue, although price promotions may well still feature, obvious examples include Harrods and Gucci.

Price competition

Price competition carries significant risks. When the big chains engage in a price war competitive advantage

When the big chains engage in a price war competitive advantage is gained for a short time only.

is gained for a short time only. Price matching too can be a dangerous activity, whenever you match a competitor's price it sends out a distinct message about your other prices.

Everyday low prices (ELP or EDLP)

Everyday low pricing is an interesting modern pricing technique. It's also the best example of the failure of slavish dedication to a rigid price proposition. The theory of ELP is that every price in store is as low as possible every day. Furthermore that prices will not be slashed during sale periods, indeed that there will be no more sales at all just the lowest prices every day.

US-based Wal-Mart are often credited as the pioneer of ELP. Founder Sam Walton would almost certainly have suggested that all Wal-Mart did was to take discounting and direct-from-manufacturer purchasing further than his competitors.

In the early 1990s Kingfisher companies – at the time, B&Q, Woolworths, Superdrug and Comet – were among the first adopters of ELP in the UK. Others have since followed. Some retailers have always believed consistently low prices to be an honest customer proposition but have never felt the need to claim subscription to an evangelist philosophy.

The strongest myth surrounding the British interpretation of ELP is that offering everyday low pricing precludes the use of traditional price promotions. This interpretation of the technique is wrong. Not just wrong, it is an anti-competitive advantage because it ties one hand behind the retailer's back. I worked for Comet when the company first introduced ELP. A Kingfisher finance team attempted to codify ELP into a philosophy and then to interpret it as a mission, applicable to the whole business. Pricing became the absolute focus of what we, as a retailer, did. Actually the mission at Comet was, or should have been: 'To sell a great range of electrical goods to delighted customers'. Pricing is an element of that mission but so are fantastic, surprising and exciting promotions. To make pricing the absolute mission was wrong. It did not provide competitive advantage.

To make pricing the absolute mission is wrong.

I am always mis-trustful of attempts to shoehorn simple common sense into complex strategy. At Comet we interpreted ELP as meaning all prices would be monitored against those of major competitors, then adjusted to match or beat these price points. In addition each key product category would feature at least one product priced lower than any entry price-point offered by our competitors. The product would then remain at that category-killing low price everyday. So, for example, we offered a 14″ portable colour TV at £99 when the previous entry price-point for this product was £109. All our competitors were at the £109 price when Comet introduced the category killing £99 TV set. For how long do you suppose that competitive advantage lasted? A year? A season? Well Dixons, Currys and Argos cut their price point to match ours within weeks. All that happened was the whole sector now made £10 less profit for every one of those 14″ televisions sold. That's £10 lost out of gross margin don't forget.

Because we at Comet were committed to our mis-interpretation of ELP it made it very hard to respond in turn to our competitor's actions. If we dropped our own price further it would have damaged the credibility of our ELP proposition suggesting that our previous price was not the lowest every day price after all. If we remained at £99, just like everyone else, we had no competitive advantage since pricing was our only competitive lever. Building the mission around ELP provided no competitive advantage at all. Yet ELP is still the focus at Comet today. Their current strapline is 'Home of Low Prices, Look No Further.' Actually if you do look further then you can sometimes find products on Comet's own website for sale at a lower cost than in store! The same product! In the summer of 2002 a particular Philips Widescreen TV could be had for £50 less by ordering off the Comet website rather than buying it in store.

That 'Look no further' line should tell you what really sits behind the fashion for ELP propositions. When rivals' store environments, prices and product ranges are so similar there is a terrible fear that a customer will simply walk from store to store and buy on price alone. Comet, as do many others, believe that convincing the customer that their prices are always reliably low will ensure the customer only comes to them. I'm not sure that's very realistic given the amounts being spent on a single electrical product. Would you only check one store when spending £600 on a telly? ELP, as practised by many is fatally flawed.

Merchant dealing

I put the challenge of the £99/£109 14″ TV to a number of Britain's best retailers. They decided quickly that it would have been much more effective to have taken that TV and to have slashed a genuine deep cut off the price, say to £89, and then to have run that as a limited stock promotion. We would have negotiated a larger order with our original equipment manufacturer (OEM) and taken a bigger discount. That stock would make up the limited promotion. The promotion would then have been presented honestly to customers: 'here's a fantastic deal we've negotiated specially for you, once its gone, its gone'. Indeed this is exactly how Asda and Tesco have been beating the electrical retailers at their own game.

Yes the competition would still match our price but by then we would have enjoyed at least two weekends of price leadership in this category. Also competitors would be forced to cut their margins from existing stock bought at their usual cost price so their profit per unit would actually be less than ours.

This bargain £89 TV would feature heavily in local press and radio advertising. Customers flicking through the local paper would see a bold, bright, honest advert. Many customers would bring forward an intended purchase as a result 'Lets get one now and put it away for Tommy's Christmas prezzy?' and 'You've been on about a telly for the kitchen, shall we get one while this cheap deal is on?' And a significant number of customers would switch to Comet for this purchase because:

1 We made it easy for them.

2 We gave them a good reason to act now instead of tomorrow.

I strongly believe that real competitive advantage comes from maintaining honest everyday prices mixed with bargains. Quite simply, not ripping off the customer, and retaining the ability to offer great, customer-delighting, promotions. It is this approach, call it a philosophy if you want, that will enable your store to convince customers that you are honest people to do business with and that you are capable of exceeding their expectations on price.

Value and bargains – the real ELP

Wander round the Wal-Mart near Hicksville (honest, it's on Long Island and I couldn't resist driving through a US town with a name like that) and you will see the pioneers of ELP doing ELP properly. It is not the rigid UK ELP approach but something much more instinctive. Yes almost every product line is on the shelf at a reliably low price. But what shines out from these everyday low-priced products are the mountain piles of Wal-Mart special promotion at exceptional low prices. Such promotions drive customer traffic very effectively. Actually the customers' belief that Wal-Mart will always present them with exciting bargains is enough to drive traffic.

In 2003 T.K. Maxx ran a poster campaign that included the strap-line 'Get a buzz from a bargain.' That is retail genius, real knowing-your-customer genius. It summarises precisely the feeling customers derive from finding a special deal. A Harrods customer is as keen on a bargain as one of the Virgin Megastore's is. The millionaire enjoys being able to boast that he got a free diamond set into the face of his new Rolex Oyster, just as much as does the ordinary person who has just saved £6 by buying two chart CDs at the same time. That is what Wal-Mart and T.K. Maxx are tapping into: the buzz customers get from beating the system, from getting a real bargain. Systemised ELP doesn't do that. All customers love bargains, we are living in a bargain driven culture.

Making bargains the star

Even in a chain-store branch where you don't get to dictate prices you can still make bargains the star. There are always awesome offers in the price lists – these might be end-of-line items or even regular stock. Try pulling lots of the end-of-line product into your store from other stores around the company and then putting them out there in front of customers. Don't forget clearance and manager's specials too as bargains.

Make up some simple flyers featuring these star bargains. Hand these out on the car park and around town. If you have the budget get them delivered with the local free papers too. Have your team point out the specials to every customer who comes through the door: 'just in case you're in the market for X later I wanted to tell you we have got them at Y price for a week or until the stock runs out'. That's not pushy, it is friendly no-pressure selling.

Enthuse the whole team at your daily team meetings. Tell them about the day's top three bargains. Consider running a little incentive on those lines; a bottle of champagne goes to the person who sells the most over the weekend. A bottle of bubbly is just enough to help the team take notice, it's a welcome treat for most, but it's not so much that sales people will mis-sell just to get it. Put flyers on doors and on the counter-top. Set up an A-frame outside if you can. Sometimes the council take offence to the presence of these A-frames but you won't know until they send you a nice letter and ask you to take it down, so go ahead and see what happens!

The combination of honest pricing and real bargains will boost your reputation and your sales.

Pulling together the bargains is hard work. You must be inventive, on top of your inventory, and ready to act fast. The work is worth it, you will drive customers into your store and the combination of honest pricing and real bargains will boost your reputation and your sales. Bargains give you competitive advantage.

9

Promote or die

Happy people

Carefully considered promotions can do masses for the business, and in conjunction with honest pricing are essential performance improvement tools. There are of course those other factors to consider. Promotions in isolation from great customer service or attention to employee needs are near worthless. Poor, aggressive or sneaky promotions may bolster sales short term but unhappy customers will rarely come back (breaking Rule 3 of the four Rules of Performance Improvement – Persuade existing customers to return to your store more often) and will tell friends how rubbish you are (breaks Rule 1 – Sell to new customers). Unhappy employees will leave (that has a cost to you so breaks Rule 4 – Improve margin by cutting overheads and improving sales quality) or will not make any active selling efforts (breaking Rule 2 – Sell more in each transaction).

27 Promotions

Here I have listed most of the popular promotion options open to retailers. I've included a table that makes it easy to see which promotions are good for achieving better performance under each of the four improvement rules. Finally the promotions planner will help you to see what promotions are right for you and when to run them.

1 Joint activity

Look for promotions you can share with either manufacturers or other retailers in your street. The obvious benefit is that you can pool costs and then afford to promote the activity more aggressively. An example of retailers engaging in joint activity might be a 'fun day' held within your shopping centre. A manufacturer and retailer joint activity could include manufacturer-supplied demonstrators, linked to a customer promotion and a manufacturer-funded staff incentive.

2 Displays in empty stores

I'd like to credit Rick Segel 'one of the highest rated retail speakers in the world' with this brilliant idea. Find the landlord of an empty local retail unit and offer to put a display in the window. It makes the unit look more appealing for the landlord to rent and provides you with an excellent advertising space.

3 Sponsorship and community events

Don't always dismiss requests for sponsorship right out of hand. Sometimes a sensible sponsorship can do more for you than, say, your Yellow

Picture: Koworld

So long as they walk out with a bag!

Pages advert. Businesses located at the centre of smaller communities gain most benefit from this form of promotion. Sponsoring events such as the town fun run or village fête makes a very strong statement about your commitment to the community. Many retailers have reported that the goodwill this creates does translate into sales.

4 Adverts in changing rooms

Cheap, easy and brilliant: put adverts in your changing rooms. Your customer is absolutely captive when they are in there and they have plenty of time to read. Think especially about featuring deals on accessories. Customers who bite will be helping to push up your average transaction values.

5 Children's competitions

Maybe we are just a nation of soppy souls but children's competitions always work well. These can be very simple colouring competitions or letter writing. Perhaps themed 'draw or write a letter about your Mum for Mother's Day'. Local papers love this sort of thing. You have a good chance of getting a photo printed in the paper of the winner in your store.

6 Tip sheets

No matter what your product you can easily produce useful tip sheets. A sheet of tips might seem a little uninspiring perhaps but time and again retailers tell me that customers go nuts for these, often citing the tip sheets as the reason why customers come back. You can write tip sheets yourself or have a well-known expert do them for you at a cost. Formats can be anything from a full colour booklet to a small card fixed to a shelf edge. My favourite format is loose A5 so that customers can take the tip sheets away with them. Here are some forms of tip sheets:

▶ Recipes in a grocers.

▶ Recommendations and explanations in a wine merchants.

▶ Hi-fi reviews in an electrical retailer.

▶ Home projects in a DIY store.

▶ Album reviews in a music shop.

7 Loyalty programmes

I don't believe that customers are ever loyal to the over-hyped special offers, magazines or bits of tinsel that most loyalty programmes consist of. In my wallet is a Nectar Card, a Tesco Club Card and a WHSmiths Club Card. However I'll happily spend money in Asda, buy a paper from my pal Ali round the corner or get a book in Waterstones. I'm not loyal even though I am in the loyalty programme. Neither am I alone in that response, few of these loyalty programmes really work. Customers are loyal to great friendly service, honest prices and nice places to shop not to a plastic card.

The kind of loyalty programmes that do work are usually much simpler. Maybe a coffee house gives you a little card that they stamp each time you visit, and that entitles you to your sixth coffee free. Or a pizza company offers a loyalty bonus that allows you to get any pizza you want for free if you have saved up four receipts from previous orders. Those kind of loyalty programmes are unobtrusive, relatively low cost and customers really like them.

8 Customer-get-customer

You could offer existing customers a gift, store vouchers perhaps, if they recommend your store to a friend who then makes a purchase. All you need is a printed coupon which you give to every customer with their till receipt. The customer can fill in this coupon and give it to their friend. The friend brings in the coupon and it has the original customer's details still written on it so you can send them their reward.

If you are confident that people like you enough to recommend your store to friends this is an effective way in which to make it easy for them to do exactly that.

9 Buy one get one free (or two-for-one, three-for-two, etc.)

In 2003 this was the UK's most popular promotional mechanic. If you can afford to run them, run them. Promote such offers heavily. Talk to your suppliers about funding either the offer, the advertising or both! If you can run a steady stream of good offers over a long period then this becomes even more effective because customers begin to pop in just to see what you've got on 'special'.

10 Sampler clubs

In some ways this is an extension of the tip sheet idea but with a chance for customers to actually try the product out. You take a group of your customers and sign them up to a hands-on sampling club. In that hi-fi store example you could hold regular demonstration evenings just for members, hold set-up lessons with an expert, make pre-ordering on limited edition products available to the members first, and run exclusive offers.

11 Percentage off

Exactly what it says, you run either a day where everything is, say 10 per cent off, or you reduce a selection of lines for a limited period of time. It has become very hard to make such events really work though. The DIY sheds especially have trained customers to think that anything less than a 25 per cent discount isn't worth their while. Percentage-off promotions also make a negative statement about your usual prices.

Marking down individual clearance or special purchase products is fine. These special bargains really fire-up your customers.

12 Special nights

Inviting selected customers to join you in the store for an exclusive evening of demonstrations and offers can be very effective. Provide refreshments and snacks and if appropriate bring in a relevant speaker and entertainment too. Try to pick a theme or a special reason for doing it because that can help you to promote the night more effectively. A sports shop for example could invite customers in to celebrate Sven Goran Erikssons' birthday. Its frivolous sure but gives you a hook too. This is another one that can get you coverage in the local paper.

13 Surveys

You should be asking customers for their views anyway but surveys can also be used as promotional tools. Create a survey and then mail it to members of your data base. Include a 'thank you' voucher for a discount in store. It reminds customers you are there, it tells them customer satisfaction is important to you and it gives them a reason to come and shop with you.

14 Celebrity visit

Getting a celebrity into your store for a PA (public appearance) can be fantastic for generating traffic. They are not always as expensive as you might think either; TV actors especially if they live locally, can be a bargain! You can find the contact details of almost all British-based actors in a book called *Spotlight*. Your town library will have a copy. Make sure you tell customers and the local paper that this is happening.

15 Book signings

You don't have to be a bookshop to hold book signings. A fishing tackle shop can get just as much benefit from having the captain of the British Coarse Fishing Team in to sign his new book. In fact it's sometimes a good way for a non-bookseller to get a celebrity in without having to pay them. Heavily promoting the event is key to making a book signing really work for you.

16 Lunch at the store

People are so busy today that lunchtime often becomes a trade-off between eating or shopping. Another idea from the US is to help your customers to do both. Think about putting on a simple open-packaged lunch for every customer who visits you on one day or one week of lunchtimes. Obviously it's worth avoiding greasy or staining food. Leafleting local offices is the best way to promote these events. Word is that they are really very effective at getting new people into your store.

17 Seminars, 'how tos' and in-store events

Absolutely essential whatever your business. Get local traders, designers and even manufacturers' reps in to show off your products and show what to do with them. Construct a series of seminars, 'how tos' and in-store events and then give every customer a calendar with these marked on. Seminars attract customers and they help customers to decide to spend more money. 'How to' demonstrations and events such as fashion shows bring theatre and drama into your store. That excites customers and helps to make their experience of your store a much more enjoyable and interesting one.

18 Meeting place

If you have a training room or large office that is not fully utilised consider offering it to local businesses as an outside meeting space. This creates massive goodwill and hardly anyone currently does it, which will mean you will stand out. Maybe invest in a coffee maker, cups and a lick of paint to make the place attractive. Check your insurance terms as well, just in case.

19 Charity giving

An honest charity promotion is a winner in many sectors. It works especially well if you have an older customer base. Mature customers tend to be the most receptive to support a charity. The usual format would be to partner with a particular charity and then agree to donate a stated percentage of profits earned during a specific special charity day.

20 Local radio outside broadcasts

If you have got the space, offer to let the local radio station come and do an OB (outside broadcast) from your car park or store. Make it coincide with a strong event and you'll find the stations quite keen to be involved.

21 Banded product

This is a cousin of the buy-one get-one free offers. Banding is usually applied to fast-moving lines and means either attaching a different product to another for free, or putting two products together as a package deal. It's a good way to move a slower line out with a more popular one and to please the customer at the same time.

22 Discount off future purchase

I am a big fan of this technique, also sometimes called delayed discount. Every customer buying on the promotional day gets a money-off voucher that they can use in the store on another day. Usually the value of the voucher depends on the value of the original spend, so a typical offer might look like this:

▶ Spend £20 get a £5 voucher off next purchase

▶ Spend £50 get a £12 voucher off next purchase

▶ Spend £100 get a £30 voucher off next purchase.

You can afford to be quite generous because a high proportion of the vouchers you give out will never be redeemed. Incidentally make sure that whatever you use is secure and that it has an expiry date and a 0.0001p cash equivalent mark on it.

Promote it on the day with lots of bold signs and make sure you have told all your data base contacts to come visit. This promotion type makes a great story for advertising too.

23 Gift certificate promotions

Very similar to the discount off future purchase offer, except redeemed using normal store gift certificates which can be used at any time. Customers treat gift certificates more like money so redemption rates, and cost too, will be much higher.

24 Buy now pay later

A credit product based promotion. Very popular among big-ticket retailers because it enables customers to fulfil tomorrows desires today! Actually they are a good deal for both punter and retailer. These promotions don't carry perhaps the same excitement and call to action that they once did though. Customers are used to seeing them now.

25 Interest free credit

Very powerful promotion that enables customers to buy your product and pay for it in instalments without them incurring any credit interest. Various deals are available to suit independent retailers and are worth serious consideration if you are aiming to move big-ticket items.

26 Storecard

Storecards earn us retailers a lot of money, and they can be very convenient for some customers. I struggle with storecards though from an ethical standpoint. This is a very expensive form of credit with interest rates that are way above those for ordinary credit cards or for personal loans. Lots of good ordinary people, our customers, get caught out by storecards and they run up huge debts with awful consequences. Retail is a people business, I don't believe we should be responsible for making anyone's life more difficult. So for that reason I cannot recommend running a storecard.

27 Bargains

And finally, the most powerful promotion of all: the humble bargain. Customers love bargains. So much so that I have filled this book with thoughts on how to get hold of, promote and sell bargains in your store. Scour your

Customers love bargains.

price lists, badger your suppliers, pester the marketing team, gather-up end of lines or last season's stock and go mental for your customers. Bargains bring people in, they make them spend more and they bring them back again.

Case study 9.1 Wall 'o' video at WHSmith

Piling high and selling cheap is still a great promotional method. Christmas of 2002 and you could not move in WHSmith stores for 5-packs of blank TDK VHS videotapes, offered at a good but not remarkable price. It was a buy-one-get-one-free deal. Few people actually need ten blank videotapes at once though. Blank videotapes are ugly and they are massive; people tolerate the need for them, they don't desire them. Frankly this promotion struck me as a difficult sell.

Managers dealt with this challenge differently. In some stores I saw dump bins dotted around, others had them on whole length shelves. I don't know if this was an idea the team at WHSmith Croydon had themselves or if there were other stores merchandised in the same way but here they had a solution that really caught my eye. They had built a three foot high wall of these tapes and snaked it all around a large central island-style cash desk. They had worked the wall such that it also made a neat Christmas queue guide. The wall 'o' tapes was probably visible from the moon, it was certainly visible from all parts of the store.

I watched customers queue; they just could not help themselves from touching the tape packs. After absent-mindedly picking a pack up many, many customers then went on to pick up another and buy them. I was very pleased to see the wall shrinking every time I went in to the store. I bet if we looked at the Croydon team's numbers it would show a massive volume of those video tapes shifted, and I'm certain it would be a greater volume than was sold in any of the other stores with dump bins or tapes on shelves. This kind of lateral display thinking can do wonders for your success with promotions.

Table 9.1 Promotions and the rules of performance improvement at a glance

	1 Sell to new customers	2 Sell more in each transaction	3 Persuade customers to return to your store more often	4 Cuts overheads and improve sales quality
The scale runs 0 to 10, 0 = No effect, 5 = Neutral effect, 10 = Very powerful effect				
1 Joint activity	7	3	1	8
2 Displays in empty stores	5	0	5	8
3 Sponsorship and town events	4	0	10	4
4 Adverts in changing rooms	0	10	6	6
5 Children's competitions	0	5	7	5
6 Tips sheets	8	6	8	9
7 Loyalty programmes	0	5	10	3
8 Customer-get-customer	8	5	6	5
9 Buy one get one free	8	7	10	2
10 Sampler clubs	1	5	10	7
11 Percentage-off	6	7	6	3
12 Special nights	6	7	7	5
13 Surveys	6	0	8	6
14 Celebrity visit	10	0 or 10*	8	2
15 Book signings	8	0 or 10*	8	8
16 Lunch at the store	7	0	8	5
17 Seminars and 'how to' events	8	10	10	6
18 Meeting place	7	0	8	6
19 Charity giving	6	0	6	3
20 Local radio outside broadcasts	6	0	6	8
21 Banded product	8	5	8	7
22 Discount off future purchase	7	7	10	5
23 Gift certificate promotions	8	5	10	5
24 Buy now pay later	7	5	7	4
25 Interest free credit	8	6	8	5
26 Storecards	2	8	7	10
27 Bargains	10	10	10	5

* A celebrity or author who is expert in the same field as the store can lead customers into buying all sorts of extras to go with a base purchase, a non-related one can't!

Promotions planner

Putting together a promotions planner is simple but essential

1   Start with 12 sheets of A4, one for each month of the year.

2   Write in all the things you can predict will be happening, for example a January sale.

3   Write down all the predictable quiet times for your business – summer holidays might be one.

4   Write in all the predictable mad times such as Christmas.

5   Add any product launches that you know of.

6   Write in any major events that could offer some good promotion links, the Olympics or a blockbuster movie perhaps.

7   Now you will have a good idea of where you have either dead zones to fill, or mad times to either avoid or strengthen, and you can see where some themed promotions might work well.

Choosing the right promotions is an art but this information can really help you. For example, if your business is quiet during August because of summer holidays that's because most people are away, it might be sensible then to run promotions that maximise transaction values – pull more cash in from the few customers you do have at that time.

You can easily use a template of these planners to impress your potential new bosses at interviews too.

Learning from hardcore street retailers

One of the most effective lessons in retail can be learned by taking a walk into one of the really hardcore selling environments. Scenarios where customers are transient and pitches are furious. The two that best illustrate these situations are outdoor markets and consumer shows.

One of the best of these lessons can be had for free just by walking down the Whitechapel Road at lunchtime. This stretch of East London highway is home to a permanent street market. The traders here compete to sell clothes, food, CDs of questionable authenticity, electronics and homewares. There is even one guy there who sells beds. Six foot beds, bunk beds, lots of them, on display, on a little market stall!

I'd like you to take a look at

1   Vocal promotion.

2   Merchandising.

3   Pricing logic.

4   Demonstration.

1 Vocal promotion

Traders' calling out to punters can be exhilarating to watch, especially when it's done well. What you can learn from observing is a sense of what really turns customers on. The lines shouted out have been passed down from trader to trader over generations. Traders still use them because they work. Go beyond the old-time vocal theatricals and you can see some incredible promotional instinct at work. But you don't have to shout you can let your POS do that for you. Consider how you might transfer some of that into your store POS.

2 Merchandising

When I walked the Whitechapel Road in February of 2003, lychees were the big popular draw offered by grocers there. The market contains six grocers' stalls each offering similar products, although one uses specialism very effectively by featuring a display of hard-to-find Bangladeshi cooking ingredients. It was the merchandising of lychees on these very busy grocery stalls that was so interesting. Lychees were all presented at the front of each stall, right out in the flow of customers. If these were normal high street shops then the lychees would be on the pavement outside the imaginary shop's doors. Each pallet of lychees was presented still stacked on a delivery trolley. At first I thought this was just because the fruits were in the middle of actually being delivered. Next day though the lychees were again right out front on their delivery trolleys.

I asked stallholder Dinesh why he did this. 'Its freshness' said Dinesh and went on to say that customers who saw the lychees tended to believe the fruits were really fresh because they hadn't been around long enough to be taken off the delivery trolley. 'How fresh are they?' I asked. 'Three days these ones.' 'Do your customers believe your lychees are fresh every morning?' 'Yeah, they do.'

What the story of the lychees illustrates is two brilliant merchandising rules

1   Perception is an astonishingly powerful customer motivator.
2   Prominent positioning of hot items hooks customers.

Case study 9.2 Cargo call-birds

Homewares store Cargo used another hot item in the same way. Right in the entrance and usually visible from a side window, most stores would feature a massive display of bargain-priced tea lights: a couple of quid for a bag of 100. They look great in the display, the cost is bargain basement and people always need tea lights. Customers would spot them from the road, grab a bag and then have to walk through the store to pay for them. Cargo then enjoyed the benefit of the additional purchases that customers picked up on that walk to the cash desk. Such a simple little thing and every store should do it.

---

3 Pricing logic

The pricing logic in play on market stalls looks very simple: lots of bargains to attract punters. Actually each stall has three pricing strands in place:

1   The stunningly cheap, prominently placed 'call-birds'. An example might be 'Three T-shirts £4'.
2   Ticket prices – what is shown on the hand-written price tags and signs.
3   Negotiated prices – the price after haggling.

The negotiated price offers an excellent lesson in deal making. Something more complex than simple haggling is going on. Ask the guy who runs the clothes stall for his cash price on a £15 pair of jeans and his reply isn't '£14 mate' it is a much cleverer 'I'll do you two pair for £25'. Push him a bit further and he might go on to chuck-in a free belt too. Instead of just falling over and giving in to your demand for a discount he has ensured that he turns stock around faster and increases his average transaction value. A calculator-like understanding of his margins helps in those on-the-spot deals but you can teach all your staff to do this too. I've shown how to do this in the following 'Creating Sale Closers' section.

4 Demonstration

Demonstration is a phenomenally powerful promotional tool. Watch the stallholders closely. They handle the product constantly; rotating CD titles to the front, shifting clothes, rearranging sizes or colours, juggling sweets, playing music, sparking-up toys, cooking-up spices on their hot-plates. Almost every grocer you see will actually hold a bag of product in his hand as he barks out the deal on that item. At consumer shows this becomes even more overt where sales people draw crowds by putting on displays of their product's prowess.

Another great training ground for learning demonstration skills and I am serious, is the shopping channel on cable and satellite TV. Watch especially the guest presenters. These are the people from the product manufacturers who get to come on to the show and plug their wares. These men and women are brilliant, instinctive performers who talk and demonstrate benefit after benefit. Imagine how effective this type of demonstration can be in your store.

> **Customers are drawn to products when they see life and action around them.**

What I'm suggesting you do here is to tap in to power of every day performance. The demonstrating, playing with, almost, of products. Customers really are drawn to products when they see life and action around them. Helping customers to more-easily imagine your product actually working for them is very powerful. Demonstration does two really significant and useful things for you:

1   Draws customers' attention.

2   Makes the store environment feel more dynamic.

Both these effects will boost sales.

Making it stick

Over and over we have talked about how the best of retailing is down to common sense, passion and gut feel. Out on the streets, on the market stalls, at the consumer shows, these components of success are in plentiful supply. They can be seen in the way stallholders price, merchandise, promote and demonstrate. All of the lessons on display can be learned and applied to your store, whether that is a hole-in-the-wall grocers or a 25,000 square foot Currys.

The lychees off Dinesh's stall were delicious by the way. He said that the ones I bought were fresh that morning. So I bought two tubs and as a special deal he did me some kiwi fruit half price too: lovely.

Creating sale closers

Stall holders' instinctive deal-making ensures they turn stock faster and critically that they increase average transaction values. Pushing up the value of each sale is the key to increasing business performance. Helping your team to make better packages is also a very effective way to control store discount levels because you can move away from those profit-eating 'I'll do you a 10 per cent discount off the package' moments.

In effect what we are looking to achieve is a menu of packages that sales assistants can choose from to close sales with. The customer never sees the package deal menu, only the sales person does. This is because you want the customer to feel that the deal in front of them has been built especially for them and for them only. That uniqueness is important because it helps the customer to feel that they have beaten the system. That they have achieved something special because they thought to ask for a discount. Having the menu ready but hidden is not a deception, rather it's just a sensible way to ensure a smooth transaction.

Building the packages

First step is to ask the team to suggest some package deals they think might help them to do the job better.

Examples of package deals

▶ If you want to take a second pair of trousers with that suit then I can let you choose a free tie as well.

▶ Lets do the matching DVD player as well as the TV, that way I can offer a free delivery and maybe half-price on a couple of DVD movies.

▶ Since this dress is for a special occasion I can offer you the shoes at 25 per cent off if you'd like to take a matching bag as well.

▶ I can't discount the designer frames but I can do you a similar shape in our own brand and a pair of prescription sunglasses for £10 less than the designer frames on their own, how does that sound?

Once you've identified some packages it is then time to explore the numbers. Experience proves that sharing information on margin can have a positive effect on the team. They appreciate being 'in the loop' and they tend to go on to become more aware of where the best profits are to be had. So now is a good time to discuss high-margin/low-margin products with the team.

Some of the packages suggested will feature products that are already at such a low margin that you cannot afford to discount them at all, no matter how large the potential sale. Be honest with the team about such products.

Of the packages on the table you must now prioritize. Which do the team truly believe will make a real difference to the sales experience? It is vital that you judge these packages from the customer perspective.

Ask questions that put you in the customer's role

▶ Would a deal like this make me feel good about the store?

▶ Am I excited by what's on offer?

▶ Is this combination really useful to me?

▶ Does it do what I want?

If you can answer 'yes' to customer questions like these then the deal has jumped its first hurdle.

Do the maths

Work it out with the team. Keeping them involved right now is important. They will feel greater ownership of the end result than if you had instead thanked them for their ideas and promised to get back to them.

Base your package deal proposals on

1   Margin and usual discount range

2   Stock turn around

3   Average transaction value

4   Realism.

1 Margin and usual discount range

What do we need to make, as a percentage, from a combo like this one? If your usual discount range is 2 per cent and you feel this package will need a 10 per cent overall discount (counting money-off, free product, free after-sales or delivery, etc.), then you must help the team to understand that the extra 8 per cent will need to be saved elsewhere. It is a good time to bring home the reality of the impact discounts have on margin.

2 Stock turn-around

Adding a slow-selling line as a free item for a package sale helps you enormously. You can also afford to be a little more generous when calculating the overall discount. Remember to keep the customer in mind. If the slow line is slow because it is rubbish, unattractive or naff then you will just annoy the customer by suggesting it as a deal sweetener. Also if the main item in the suggested package is in short supply then the team clearly should not be offering any discount on it at all.

3 Average transaction value

Work this out as a percentage. If the proposed deal will create a sale that is double your usual average transaction value then it is worth being relatively generous. Raising average transaction values, while maintaining healthy margins is the key to increasing store performance.

4 Realism

Don't get carried away. If you cannot see a need for a particular package then say so. Explain your reasoning clearly and invite comment. It can be tempting for a sales person to see 'deal making' just as an opportunity for them to make their life a lot easier. Remember package deals are for one purpose only: to turn a request for discount into a larger sale. To make a sale that is good for you and good for the customer.

Write the deals up

By now you will have a very strong list of package deals. Issue this list to the team. Two weeks later review the list. Which deals are working? Which need adjusting? Any new ideas? What's been the effect on overall discounts and on margin? Have we been over generous? Are there areas where we can be even bolder?

Public promotion opportunities

Are any of our package deals so effective that we should 'go public' with them and set-up proper promotions? Select a member of the team to be responsible for turning the best three packages into public promotions. Ask them to pull together a promotions plan and then put it into action!

10

Marketing for real people

Tell me what it is, why I'd want one and how to get it. That's all I give a monkey's about. If you can do that in a humorous, dramatic or otherwise attention grabbing way then fine – knock yourself out. Please don't talk to me in Latin, black and white, obtuse images or stuff that goes way over my head because I just don't care enough about you or your product to bother trying to understand your clever rubbish.

In that one paragraph you have all the rules of advertising you will ever need. Be clear, tell people what the benefit to them is and then make it very easy for them to buy from you. Ad agencies argue that advertising is about building brands too. There is some truth in this but frankly brand is built more powerfully by your shop, your people in it and your store culture. Slick eye-candy advertising is simply not important.

easyJet and Richer Sounds have two of the ugliest logos I have ever seen but it makes not one little tiny bit of difference. easyJet do cheap flights with no fuss, people fly with them because getting a packet of peanuts and paying twice as much to some other airline is daft. To make it easy for people to book with easyJet their telephone number is painted in five-foot-high letters on the side of their aeroplanes. Punters buy cheap honest hi-fi from Richer Sounds, the shop never rips customers off, they seem pleased to help people make decisions and they give customers a catalogue with a list of their stores on.

Both brands tell you what they are for, why you would want to use them and how to do business with them. Both those brands are sales phenomenon. Both are never going to win awards for the glossiness of their advertising.

Advertising made simple

Pot Noodle adverts are funny and they make you think about eating Pot Noodles. McDonalds' adverts make you hungry. Chrysler posters have just four big words on them '£2003 off in 2003' and they have a big picture of a car on them. These posters help you to understand that you can get that car for £2003 discount if you buy it during 2003. That is as creative as advertising ever needs to get.

When McDonalds slashed their UK advertising budget they demanded that agencies still deliver just as many 'spots' on TV, radio and posters. The only way this could be done was to cut production budgets. It forced agencies to focus on the 'this is a hamburger, they taste nice, come and buy one' aspect of the brand. McDonalds adverts have never been so effective.

Beauty has its place

There is space for the beautiful, those breathtaking adverts that force their way into your awareness. But these are very much the exception that rather prove the rule, you remember these because they are exceptional. Orange, the mobile phone network, has built a hugely successful brand without ever showing a picture of a telephone in its advertising (there was one, once, but Motorola were paying and forced the issue, but even then the phone featured was only shown as an x-ray negative). You might think this goes against the simple doctrine I've outlined here. It doesn't. Orange's adverts always tell you what they are for (mobile communications) they always focus on one clearly defined benefit at a time (say the joy of swapping pictures on a mobile), and then they put a great big phone number up on screen and suggest interested punters might like to ring to become an Orange customer.

Marketing things to make and do

Marketing is not a mythical black art, it is nothing more, or less, than a common sense framework – a framework into which adverts and promotions can be fitted. Marketing theory is actually very simple. The skill, especially in the case of retail, is not in cleverly executing the practice of marketing but rather in trusting your gut feel to keep things simple. Marketing is about understanding who your customers are, where they can be found, what they want and how much they will pay to satisfy those wants. That's really kind of it.

Marketing is about understanding who your customers are, where they can be found, what they want and how much they will pay.

The four 'P's

One of the basics of marketing theory is a simple concept called the four 'P's. It is very basic but still useful. Here they are:

Product – what are we selling?

Place – where will it be sold, how will we get it there?

Promotion – how will the product or brand be positioned and promoted in the market?

Price – how much is the product?

The four P's set up a series of questions. Who are we selling to? How do we tell them about our product? What will they pay for it? Notice how these questions form a chain? The answer to the first informs the second which in turn sets up the third and so on. Answering these questions can help you to make better decisions on promotions and on advertising.

Questions chain

1   Who wants to shop at a store like mine?

2   What is it they like about us?

3   Which products excite them?

4   What promotions do they like?

5   Where can I find these people?

6   What should I tell them?

You might want to go through these questions in a team meeting. Try to cover four or five main customer types separately. Each customer type looked at will create a slightly different thread. Use what you learn to select target audiences and to select the promotions you would like to put before them. The following pages list some of your options for reaching those audiences.

Radio

Radio is a great medium. It's very cost effective and you can paint any image you want with words. Often big and shouty words work best. Plenty of stations will help you to create your advert. Each station will also be able to give you profiles of their listeners for each of their shows. This means you can choose to advertise only on those stations, and only during those shows, listened to by people who might actually want to shop with you. There are also lots of resources available for do-it-yourself radio advertisers and that helps makes the medium very attractive.

The Radio Advertising Bureau exists 'to guide national advertisers and their agencies towards effective advertising on commercial radio.' They won't be able to advise you directly but their website is a fantastic mine of resources. Click on the truly heroic radio advert archive, all the inspiration you could ever want is there. The RAB's address is www.rab.co.uk.

TV

TV is undoubtedly a powerful advertising channel but it's expensive and it suffers a tendency to be somewhat scattergun in effect. Unless you can afford to advertise on TV lots then it's unlikely that you will reach enough of your potential customers to make this medium pay. The Advertising Association, www.adassoc.org.uk, has some useful research on its site that you might want to take a look at if you're considering TV. The channels themselves do offer advice and assistance to smaller advertisers so it is worth asking about those services. Ask too about related discounted advertising packages.

Print

Clear bold messages work best and buy the largest portrait spot you can afford. Don't do national if you are local. Don't be seduced by glamorous graphics. A bold typographical treatment highlighting a great promotion accompanied by a shot of your product is more effective.

Posters

Traditional large-format posters can act like a second storefront but they are expensive. These days anything that doesn't move seems to be available for placing an advert on – everything from posters in pub toilets to the handles of petrol pumps. Maiden is the largest independent outdoor media owner in the UK and worth talking to if you are interested in exploring posters. Their web address is www.maiden.co.uk.

Catalogues

A catalogue can be a single flyer or a 32-page colour extravaganza. Never underestimate the power of catalogues. They provide you with huge scope to tell people about your fantastic deals and at the same time talk about why your store is a nice place to visit and to do business with. George Whalin, one of America's most effective retail consultants, suggests that 'if you have one item and just one page, that's a catalogue, start from there and build it over time'.

Catalogues are exciting because there is so much you can do with them. You can hand them out as flyers, you can put them into the local free papers, you can mail them to your customer data base and you can give them out to visitors to your store. There are two existing catalogues that I suggest you take a look at as they represent excellent examples of what you can achieve.

1 Ikea

Take a look in the back section where they focus on a small number of special deal items. It is stunning the way that such a simple but strong presentation can make something like a £3 stool look so utterly desirable. The room sets too, though expensive to create and photograph, are excellent.

What they do so effectively is make suggestions to the customer. Readers see a nicely dressed bed in a lovely room and they want one.

2 Richer Sounds

This is how to do catalogues! Masses of deals, a front cover full of 'wow' offers, a selection of 50p traffic-builder promotions promoted up front, and lots and lots of text talking about why Richer Sounds is a great place to come and buy bargain hi-fi from. This catalogue makes you want to buy stuff.

Getting them out there

Consider how you might distribute your catalogue. Piles in the store are fine, a stand outside is better. Having a colleague hand them out on the car park or up and down the street is always worth doing. Paying a delivery person to distribute catalogues door-to-door is useful too. Of course this is also dependent on the type of catalogue you have gone for. If yours is thick, heavy and expensive then distribution will have to be more limited. Similarly, if you know that your customer falls into a very narrow interest group then you should consider distributing your catalogue directly to them, a baby goods store might want to have its catalogue in the waiting area of the local maternity ward for example.

Easy ABC data base marketing

Every store can, and must, build a customer data base. Used sensibly they drive customers into your store like no other advertising tool can. You don't need complex software, or high-powered PCs to run them, any data base programme such as Microsoft's® Access will do. You can even get by fine using just the contacts bit of the free programme Outlook Express (again available from Microsoft®). A card index will suffice in high-ticket selling situations where you are servicing a small number of prospect customers.

Data base communication can be especially useful when you find yourself competing in a sector where price differentials are slim and where promotional advantage is quickly eroded. A strong example of why can be found in videogame retail. On the UK high street Woolworths, Game, Gamestation, WHSmiths, Dixons, Virgin and HMV dominate. Take a quick walk down your high street and you will see mostly identical pricing. There might be some variation in the package deals for the videogame consoles but the games themselves will be near identically priced in every outlet.

Game and Gamestation offer added-value in the form of pre-orders, trade-in credit for old games, bargain-priced used games and wide ranges to choose from. Both have excellent company-run data base marketing campaigns, regularly mailing out magazines (supplier funded I suspect) and special offer vouchers. If I were on the marketing team at Woolies, 'Smiths or any of the others I would respond in kind. For now though its down to you, the store manager, to create something of your own.

Take the e-mail address of every customer who buys from the videogame department. As soon as you get a stock date for a hot new game, e-mail your list with a friendly note saying what and when. If you have got an offer running tell the customer about that as well. WHSmiths recently ran a fantastic two-for-the-price-of-one offer on a line of games that had been sticking stubbornly to shelves. I missed the offer because I had stopped buying games from 'Smiths, nothing more than a house move that meant I was now closer to a branch of Game. Thousands of old WHSmiths' customers would have leapt onto this deal had they known about it. A few minutes, twice a week, on the e-mail would have made the difference.

The best e-mail marketing

How to do e-mail data base marketing really well

1   Always get permission – customers hate e-mail spam it irritates them. They respond much better to expected messages, so long as these are relevant.

2   Make sure you actually have something to say, for example:

  ▶   exclusive offer

  ▶   hard-to-get item here in stock now

  ▶   end of line special bargain

  ▶   one-off event

  ▶   exciting new line due in on x date.

3   Start the e-mail with all your headings, just titles no additional body text, for example:

▶   buy one get one free on all paperback fiction this weekend only.

▶   new Harry Potter book arrives in-store here on 11 June – reserve your copy now.

▶   David Beckham here signing his new autobiography on 1 July.

4   Remember: time limits on offers always help to drive customers into action.

5   Then in the body of the e-mail, below these headlines, you can expand on each subject. Try to keep words to a minimum, just tell the story and then get out.

▶   buy one get one free on all paperback fiction this weekend only.

▶   choose any two from our huge range of great titles and you get the cheapest free, that includes all of our current best sellers as well as the full selection of classic fiction. Saturday and Sunday only, we're looking forward to seeing you!

6   Remember, close with details of your store including telephone numbers and opening times.

7   Sign it! Customers appreciate a personal touch.

8   Remember the rules: 'Tell me what it is, tell me why I might want one, tell me how to get it'.

The Data Protection Act

If you are going to hold customer's data in a data base you must comply with the Data Protection Act. Many retailers have already notified that they wish to be registered under the act. If you have done so you are also likely to be entitled to use the data you hold for data base marketing purposes. You must check though before moving on. If you are in a chain-store branch the company may well have notified too but it can be tricky to find out. If you are lucky the marketing team will find out for you and will help you with the small number of compliance issues involved. If you are less lucky and

If you are going to hold customer's data in a data base you must comply with the Data Protection Act.

the marketing team get all stroppy then it may be worth considering notifying in the name of your individual store instead. Lots of clear advice on the whole process can be found at: www.dataprotection.gov.uk/dpr/dpdoc.nsf.

One of the key aspects of the Data Protection Act is permission. When you ask for someone's details you must tell them that you will be holding these details in a data base. You must also get their permission to send them things. Check on the www.dataprotection.gov.uk site for the latest advice on what to say and how to say it. Getting permission is good practice anyway, there is little point in taking someone's address only to send them things they don't want to see.

Postcards

E-mail is the nice, easy and cheap way to begin data base marketing. There is an excellent print alternative though that is still cost effective, especially as a tool for announcing big promotions, sales or as invites to store events. Stores in the US use postcard marketing-campaigns very effectively. In the UK Habitat get an honourable mention in this regard too as they have used postcard communications brilliantly for years.

The usual format is a large postcard where one side is given over to a full colour image and the other side is split into two halves. One of those halves is a space to put an address label and a stamp. The other half will then usually carry a coupon of some sort.

Local printers are plentiful so get three price quotes and ask to see samples. Get a fixed-cost quote and some examples. Make sure you and the printer both understand exactly what it is that you want. Short print runs are ideal as this lets you over time send lots of different messages to individual targeted groups of customers.

Selecting prospects to send your cards to needs a bit of thought. You want to avoid wastage and to maximise your chances of success. All current and recent customers who could conceivably need to visit you again should be targeted. Think carefully though, writing to someone who bought a sofa from you last week to tell them you are offering 10 per cent off sofas this week is always going to be a bad idea.

Think about your customers, do groups of them have particular things in common? Do you find yourself selling to people who all live in certain areas of town? Are your products related to their hobbies, or to their work? Are there any age groups that you seem to attract disproportionately? Looking at these factors will help you to identify other groups of people who are not yet your customers but who are very much like your existing ones. These prospect groups are almost certainly worth talking to and a postcard offer might just do the trick.

Case study 10.1 Sports promotion

Here is an example of how you might use your newly acquired understanding of who your customers are and where they come from. A sports independent, James Harris, knew from listening to his customers that a number of them were new and from a particularly well-off suburb of Chester. James asked more questions and discovered that these customers were also patrons of a health club that was running a new-member drive.

James rang the manager of the club, asked if he could pop over for a coffee and a chat about business. The value of face-to-face meetings should never be underestimated; more things get done after a handshake. During the meeting James suggested a promotion: he offered to distribute the health club's new-member offer leaflet in his store. That was an attractive proposition since James' customers were exactly those sought after by the club. In return James asked that his current postcard promotion be distributed to existing club members. He was running a neat freebies promotion; free squash tuition video with rackets, free branded sports socks with trainers, three-for-two on jogging pants – that sort of thing, mostly supplier-funded too. They agreed and both ran the promotion for three months.

James was able to track response from his perspective because, where the address label would normally go he'd put a sticker instead that showed the club name and included a space for the customer to write-in their own name and address. James reckoned he gained a good stream of new customers and all for the sake of a phone call, a chat and a box of his postcards.

Keeping track – measurement

Any direct activity needs to be made measurable. You can do this easily by adding coded coupons to printed materials, and by asking e-mail customers to quote a reference code when they come in. It doesn't matter if the customer cannot remember the code just that they tell you they want to take-up an offer you e-mailed to them.

Any direct activity needs to be made measurable.

Set up a basic Microsoft Excel spreadsheet to make tracking easy. Literally just a few columns for the dates and then a few rows for the various promotions you are running. Then record the number of people responding, the total value of their purchases and the margin earned on each transaction. At the end of each week work out the total profit accounted for by your promotions. Then deduct from that the cost of the activity you ran. So long as you capture every relevant sale then this is a crude but perfectly acceptable way to track how well each promotion is working for you.

You also need to take account of the discounts you gave to normal customers; people who would have bought from you regardless of the promotion. That is quite tricky and will often be down to your instinctive judgement. All the same it is important because this number helps you to realistically appraise returns from your efforts.

PART FOUR – **STORE**

Surprise and delight to put more money in the till

NOTE: The Grand Magasins du Bon Marche was the world's first department store. The brainchild of Aristide Boucicaut, it was established in 1852 and moved into purpose-built premises in 1869. These premises were extended in 1873 and 1876 by Louis-Charles Boileau, this latter extension being undertaken with the help of Gustave Eiffel and being notable for its use of glass and iron. This photograph: 1928.

Source: RIBA Library Photographs Collection

11

Store environment

Store layout plays a really important role in the success of your store. Whatever your format, the way in which your store is presented to your customers has a big impact on whether they decide to buy from you or not.

There are five jobs the store is doing for you

1   Tempt customers to come in.

2   Display products.

3   Show off price and promotional displays.

4   Lead customers through the different ranges.

5   Communicate your store culture.

Look and feel

It's relatively easy these days to create knock-out gorgeous stores at sensible cost. Especially as manufacturers are often rather keen to supply retailers with great looking free, or part-sponsored, display systems. Great looking is only the start; let's go through the store section-by-section.

> **It's relatively easy these days to create knock-out gorgeous stores at sensible cost.**

Windows

On the high street a good window display is critical. It must be welcoming, it must give passers by new reasons to come in and it has to be readable in five seconds. Any offers you put in the window should then be easy to locate when the customer comes in looking for them. The best spot for these is on a back wall where they can be seen from the door but require the customer to walk the whole length of your store to get there. Doing this exposes customers to more of your store increasing the potential for other sales.

New products are great as window features. When I asked the owner of a successful hardware store how he promoted his hot new items he said 'I put them in the window with a bloody great sign on them that says "bargain" and "brilliant" on it. Customers notice the sign. I know they do because they ask me about these new products and then they buy them.'

Transition zone

This is the area near the door that transfers customers from the outside and then into the store. You have an opportunity here to make or break the customer experience. If the zone is too empty customers can feel exposed and then reluctant to move further into the store. If it's too cluttered that's off-putting too because it makes it hard for customers to get in!

You also need to be aware throughout the store but here especially of what retail anthropologist Paco Underhill calls the 'butt-brush factor'. He noticed that customers hate standing anywhere that puts them at risk of other customers constantly brushing past them. In the transition zone this effect can be useful because it keeps people moving forward on into the store. In front of displays this can be a problem because you want customers to linger in those areas. When they do linger they tend to buy more often. Take a look at all the customer flows in your store, from the entrance and back out again, to see where you can make improvements.

Sales floor

You need to think about quality, shoplifting, presentation, promotion and customer flow on your sales floor. There is no magic right way to set-up your space. Have a look at Chapter 1 Reading the store. Then use this technique to shop, shop and shop again. Do it in your own store and those of successful competitors and other successful retailers. You will soon develop an appreciation of what works and what doesn't. Your eyes and your gut feel are more powerful tools in this than any pre-boxed formats can ever be.

Baskets

If yours is a store where customers ever need to pick-up more than one item then you must offer baskets. Customers who pick-up a basket nearly always buy something and very often buy more than customers who don't have a basket. Stores always benefit from having baskets available invitingly on the side edges of that transition zone.

Put the baskets higher up, not on the floor. Perching baskets on a table makes it very easy for your customers to just dangle an arm down and almost absent-mindedly pick-up a basket. Doing so will increase sales and average transaction values.

Promotional hot spots

Creative use of promotions is essential. Fill the store with them, show people excellent value and then make it easy for them to take you up on your brilliant offers. Never allow a promotion spot to go empty, if you have run out of a line, even for just a few hours, get the promotion POS off the floor right now. If you don't you will annoy customers who will feel you have let them down.

The ideal promotional hot spots

▶ visible from the door

▶ well lit

▶ bristling with stock

▶ easy to linger in front of

▶ honestly presented

▶ clearly merchandised

▶ well signed

▶ surprising.

Back wall

Do you remember how record shops always used to feature the top-twenty singles up on the back wall? That was so they could draw every customer right the way through the store. The really savvy stores would make it very easy for customers to walk through the middle of the shop to the back wall, so customers would all be flowing down that central aisle. Then when a customer had found their chosen single they would turn and look for the cash desk. This would be placed further back up towards the doors. The customer couldn't easily walk back along the central aisle because it was full of people heading towards them, so they would zigzag through the displays to either side. This zigzagging was brilliant because it meant the customer was exposed to a whole succession of promotional hot spots at the end of product racks.

Cash desk

There are lots of arguments over where best to put cash desks. To be honest all have their pros and cons. My preferred position is halfway down one side wall. You can see most of the store from there, queuing can be dealt with neatly and it doesn't eat into the best-selling areas.

Most popular options

Half-way down one side – my favourite

At the front to one side – makes it easy to greet customers walking in but puts the desk right in the middle of important promotional space

In a centre island – although islands can break up sight-lines a bit this can work really well, especially if you are able to have two people working the desk most of the time because the pair can then each watch half the store giving you full visual cover

On the back wall – popular really only because it usually puts staff near to back-of-house areas, makes it hard to greet customers and is the shoplifters' favourite option because staff are so far from the door.

Impulse buys

Whatever you sell there will be products in your range that will make great cash-desk impulse purchases. In a newsagents chocolate is an obvious example. Record shops now put band merchandise, dolls, badges and such, on counters ready for impulse purchase. Anything that is attractive, low cost and that is physically small will make a great impulse purchase. Vary your selections a little and don't crowd the till area. A few well chosen items can have a direct impact on increasing your average transaction values.

Sight-lines

Two considerations here are foremost:

1   Can customers see their way around the store?
2   Can you see them?

Customers like to be drawn through your space by the exciting and attractive products and promotions you put in their forward vision. Peripheral vision seems to be less important when customers shop. They will often miss things that are right next to them unless you lead them right to the spot.

Being able to see customers is important because it makes it easy for you and the team to acknowledge them. It is also vital in reducing shoplifting. If you can see the thief better they are less able to steal, simple as that.

Signage

Always go for crisp and readable rather than complex, over-designed or wordy. Customers just do not have the time or inclination to decipher clever complicated messages. Promotional signage especially should convey a strong bold message in just a few seconds. Tatty signage does nothing for your store, if the POS gets damaged throw it away or replace it immediately.

Customers just do not have the time or inclination to decipher clever, complicated messages.

The best store environments

A spartan plain interior suits a discount store and a jumbled-up ramshackle interior might suit a village DIY shop where staff delight in talking to people and then fetching up the right item for them. A dirty store though will almost always put customers off from even stepping inside. A smelly shop, where the products are in shabby fittings and the carpet is threadbare will put off customers.

If your store is a mess don't just complain that head office won't do anything so you can't do anything either. It is always under your control. I know a manager who would cut-up chunks of carpet from back-of-house, from under displays and then glue it down himself to replace visible worn patches. Just get it done.

I've listed below the best store environments for you to take inspiration from. I've also included a selection of stores that could be considered to be facing challenges. In this section I'm only talking about store look and feel. This is not a list of my overall favourite retailers. They can be found in Appendix B at the end of the book.

A sort of disclaimer

To maintain credibility I have only included stores in this section that I have not worked for. That way you can trust that there is no ulterior motive when I say that 'so and so' looks fab.

Best

SELFRIDGES – LONDON

Quite simply the best merchandised store in the world. The store buzzes with the energy and excitement of a Turkish bazaar while at the same time retaining the chic and style of an exclusive Bond Street boutique. The effect is thrilling – the purchase of a pack of Muji pens for £1.50 delivers the same retail therapy effect as does a £150 purchase of an Alexander McQueen shirt.

Imaginative ranging and promotional techniques play an important role in this eclectic retail palace but critical is the way in which the store has been laid out. Every floor feels different. Music and lighting is cleverly used to enhance a space or to delineate a boundary. Take a moment too to check out the sight-lines; at every important junction customers can see an uncluttered path to a selection of different but complementary store sections. For example, jump off the escalator at the menswear floor and you can see lots of exciting brands all at once but each is still distinct from the other. As you walk further into the department new brands and sections are teasingly revealed from beyond the current section. This approach ensures customers shop more of the store on each visit.

Search the store and you will notice further that standards of display, signage and cleanliness are scrupulously applied. Each concession is also encouraged to make absolute stars of a selection of its product, so for example, the excellent Alessi concession features shelf-top and table-top displays that demand customers pick-up and play with the merchandise.

BLOOMINGDALES – NEW YORK

The original Manhattan branch of this superb department store lives up to its grand billing as one of the world's best retail spaces. Many of its finest qualities are similar to those of Selfridges although it could be argued that this is a less funky atmosphere. More luxury than cool. That is probably appropriate since Bloomingdales appears to cater for a slightly more mature and certainly more conservative audience.

During a visit you'll notice the crispness of presentation, the immaculate but always approachable displays and the proliferation of aspirational brands nicely merchandised. It is the kind of atmosphere that demands you linger. Bloomingdales, and to an extent Harrods, provide us with a useful lesson in doing the basics of display well: keep it clean, uncluttered, well labelled and properly lit. Bloomingdales are also the absolute masters of store events, there is always something happening to excite customers as they walk round.

STELLA McCARTNEY – NEW YORK

Yes an expensive designer store is always going to look good given the budgets in play but this one offers some really useful transferable lessons. There are two important reasons why this store is worth looking at. The first is the way in which the designers have cleverly used changes in lighting, ceiling heights and floor levels to force customers into exploring the whole store. Just to show that I'm not an elitist snob, I'd like to point out that the bigger Currys stores do the same thing excellently too and in much the same way.

The second reason for picking out McCartney's store is the way in which displays have been made mobile. There is no carpet to fade underneath displays and all displays are either on wheels or are light enough to pick-up and move around. That means the store can be refreshed easily, essentially whenever the manager feels like it. In your case an approach like that would enable you to easily trial different store configurations. It's well worth considering this approach for application to an action zone. This is a spot where you can create excitement and buzz by changing the displays regularly and by mixing interesting promotions, offers and complementary products.

WHSMITH TRAVEL – WORLDWIDE

The travel stores are not travel bookshops as the name might suggest; these are actually the WHSmith outlets that you see at train stations and at airports. Consistency is what's most impressive about WHSmith Travel shops. Even though the retail units housing the stores are often dramatically different from each other, the branding, colours and presentation of each store are always bang-on the money, absolutely consistent. That means a customer in a hurry, as most of us are when we are in airports and stations, will spot the WHSmith very easily even through a milling throng of fellow travellers. That coupled with the reliability of the WHSmith travel offering – you always know they will have something there to make your journey more bearable – is really powerful because it makes many customers walk right past alternative kiosks just to get to 'Smiths.

Consider this strength in relation to your external branding. If yours is a chainstore ask yourself 'have I got the current signage up and are my windows helping, or hindering, my customers?' For the independents my advice on external signage is this: keep it bold, keep it simple and make it easy to read, uncluttered by unnecessary graphics or sub-headings.

The second compelling feature found in WHSmith travel outlets is, and this applies especially to the smallest ones, the ranging. Each manages to attractively display CDs, DVDs, books, papers, chilled drinks, snacks, magazines, videogames, films and batteries. Despite this wide range there is no feeling of clutter or cramping. It's an easy-to-shop store environment. They've also remembered to fit in the impulse counter items such as sweets and promotional products all of which have a positive impact on average transaction values.

VISION EXPRESS – FRANCE

The French eyecare shops are among the most attractive stores on European high streets. That's all the more remarkable when you consider how awful the previous visual presentation of Vision Express stores was. Notice the simplicity and clean lines of the excellent graphic treatment. It is simple enough to be striking without being cold and will stay in fashion for a lot longer than a more-trendy store design might have done.

Notice too the way in which staff put glasses onto customers' faces. They hold the frames by both corners, then stare intently at the customer's eyes while slipping the frames onto the face. This does two things, the eye contact establishes a powerful bond with the customer, it really does, and the whole ceremony of the placing of the frames creates a feeling of old-time-style pampering customer service. Are there products in your store that could be presented to customers for sampling in this way? Think about creating your own ceremonies of presentation. They do make a difference to the customer's perception of the service quality in your store.

Placing the lens-grinding and fitting technicians in the centre of the shop floor not only reinforces Vision Express' 'Ready in 1 hour' promise but it also adds drama and activity to the retail space. That is useful because action tends to make customers feel less like they have swum into a goldfish bowl where they are vulnerable. Instead they are subconsciously drawn in by the theatre of production. This is an important consideration in any retail space. Brits generally hate to feel exposed and will often avoid retail spaces where they feel stared at and hurried in. Watch what happens at the doors to very cool but very harshly merchandised designer stores. You will see potential customers turn to walk in, hesitate, and then think better of a trundle around the store and walk away instead. And you will see this happen regularly over a period of time.

What is your store entrance like? If it's a harsh transition zone consider placing little staging points around the entrance that lead customers into the store more gently. These staging posts can be a free standing display, something exciting attached to a pillar, anything that lets a customer move into your store a little before they then have to make the move into the store proper.

MANGO – SPAIN

Clothing stores from overseas such as Mango (Spain), Zara (Spain) and Uniqlo (Japan) are shaking up the sector in the UK. In part that is achieved by their unique approaches to store environment. Although the clothes in Mango are not expensive the way in which they are displayed makes every garment look like a million dollars. This is achieved by using simple four-armed floor-standing rails and single rail wall runs that are almost under-loaded with clothes.

Pieces are displayed on themed lines, so different colour options in a single style might appear in different parts of the store. The effect is that all the clothes are presented in a very aspirational manner. They look great and they look exclusive. The product is the star. This display logic gives customers the impression that they will be among a very few lucky buyers this season to own that exact item. It's a very powerful illusion.

The only small downside to this approach is that staff need to re-stock displays more often because the different sizes, when there may only be two of each out on the rack, disappear so quickly. For the customer the Mango stores look really different and that is important in a fashion market where customers are constantly looking for what's new and exciting.

T.K. MAXX/T.J. MAXX – WORLDWIDE

Can you think of a better way to do it? Awesome, just rack-up the bargains and let customers go mental. It works because the clothes are excellent value and they change all the time. Customers have learned that they can visit T.K. Maxx every week and find a different brilliant buy each time.

The store environment has to do nothing more than act as a shell for the bargain hunting. These stops could be in village halls and they would still work. T.K. Maxx is absolute proof of the incredible effect bargains have on customers from across a wide social-economic range. You must think about how you can use bargains to the same effect in your store, whether you are selling clothes or car parts.

POUNDSTRETCHER – UK

I love visiting Poundstretcher's head office. It's a glorious ramshackle palace of great value. Everyone there appears to practice what the company preaches 'sell customers nice things at an awesome low price'. Every office is chock full of piles of product, all are bargain finds. Incidentally the head office is attached to their distribution centre in a low-cost location outside Leeds. That shows a proper commitment to keeping overheads low so that prices to customers can remain low.

The shops themselves also reflect a thrifty attitude and are absolutely right to do so. They might use low-cost shelving and plain vinyl floor coverings but they are always clean and tidy. This is completely in-tune with the customer's perception of what Poundstretcher should be. The shops don't patronise customers either. They are what they should be – low cost environments. This honesty of presentation means it is not embarrassing to admit that you have nipped into Poundstretcher and found a bargain.

Make a realistic assessment of your own business; do you need to project an upmarket image? Or is a down-to-earth function-over-form approach more appropriate? If it is then you could well save yourself a few bob. Make sure that you then pass on that saving to the customer and so further strengthen your value positioning.

Some other store environments

FADS – UK

What is FADs? Is it a DIY store, a penny mall or a furniture store? It is really hard to tell even inside the store and little clue is offered at the window either. FADs shops are often poorly lit with harsh strip lighting doing the badly-merchandised furniture offerings little favours. Where the branches have 99p stores under the same roof they are often simply plonked at the back of the store with no signage in the window to let passers by know such a thing even exists. That is a shame because the FADs 99p offering is very strong, a talented buyer has done some great work with the range.

This is a dilemma you too must solve: just because you can see a store display doesn't mean the world sees it too. If you have a terrific secret like the FADs 99p store shout it from the front windows and from the pavement. Get some single-colour flyers printed up and hand these out on the car park and around town on a Saturday morning. If you tell customers they will come!

WOOLWORTHS – UK

The out-of-town sister format Big W is nicely presented but the high street stores are dull. There is no energy in the range or passion for value on display but surely it is value that Woolworths really stands for? Where are the breathtaking bargains? Where is the value that delights customers? Woolworths is an important store with the potential to be at the heart of our urban communities but it has to look and feel the part. Shopping at Woolworths does not feel like visiting a thrifty but fun relative, as it should do, it feels like visiting an uncle who is on his uppers. Much of that is down to the lack of real bargains but equally the store environment is playing a huge negative part.

I find their stock management hard to fathom sometimes too, what is a high street store doing showing off a huge display of 12″ terracotta plant pots?

They are big but low cost and as such eat up lots of valuable square footage. How do customers get these great awkward things home? Have you ever stood for long in Woolies and watched the customers and customer types? I have and there are significant majorities who are either with a baby in a buggy, elderly or children. How many of these people are going to be able to carry a 12″ terracotta pot home on the bus? Just exactly how much money is to be made on a low-margin low-cost pot anyway?

I'd love to see the bargains back in the store. They could use that space where the pots are (often right in the window!) to create an action zone featuring all the best mega bargains from around the store. They could then change that display every week too. It would become a space that surprises and delights customers.

The current state of the store environment at Woolworths is surprising given the fantastic strength of the business in the early 1990s when the store held market leading positions in home entertainment, toys and confectionery. This is a sleeping giant and I am not alone in looking forward to it waking up. The current senior team there is almost all relatively new into the company and this bodes well for a turnaround. That will be good for all high streets lucky enough to play host to a Woolworth's store.

MACY'S – NEW YORK

A shock awaits the customer on their first visit to 'the world's largest department store' in Manhattan. It's so disappointing and Macy's owners, Federated, should be doing more to make it great. The creaking, fussy and poorly merchandised space is ageing badly. All ten floors suffer from the effects of age. The product ranges are dull, POS is almost uniformly scruffy and the display systems are often chipped, scratched and dusty. I can remember working for area managers, back in the 1980s, who would don white gloves and run their fingers along my displays checking for dirt. Macy's would have given them all heart attacks.

This is a tragedy. Macy's has an incredible heritage, some of the most inspired buyers and marketers in retail history have worked there. The way we buy off-the-peg clothes in (almost) uniform sizes is down to a genius at

Macy's. The store can even make a strong claim to have been the first shop to have sold tea in bags! Both are innovations that helped shift more product to happy customers.

The building too has all the wonderful architectural appeal of say Harrods and the grand ground floor sales hall retains some breathtakingly beautiful detail. But when the look, feel and range is so stale architectural grandeur counts for nothing. What is more surprising is that the excellent Saks 5th Avenue and Bloomingdales are both just a short stroll away, so why not just head over and copy a little? More shocking still when you consider that Macy's and Bloomingdales are both owned by the same company.

In a not scientific poll of New Yorkers, that I conducted in Hudson's Bar, all said the same thing 'Oh Macy's is only really for the tourists, we don't go there'. and 'The Thanksgiving Day parade is cool but I don't go in the store'. My advice to Federated is this: go head-hunt Vittorio Radice the retail genius who delivered the awesome Selfridges transformation. Frankly though you could just start by hiring a good window dresser and a keen design student to redo the POS.

It would be great to see Macy's with its finger back on the retail pulse, this is a potentially wonderful store. Indeed it has been in the past. What Macy's highlights is the importance of keeping your space fresh and of the vital importance of maintaining basic standards.

The key element of surprise

Until 1852 shops were all small and specialist. That changed forever when Astride Boucicaut and his wife, Marguerite expanded their Parisian drapery store and began to sell housewares and bed linen. They called their store Bon Marché and its inception marked the birth of the world's first department store. The store launched on the back of innovations such as the promise to deliver 'to homes as far as a horse can travel in Paris', and for the first time anywhere the store featured prices clearly written on all labels. The Boucicauts are even credited with the invention of modern stock management, where rotating merchandise and the staging of summer sales, winter sales and blue-cross sales created constant change and excitement in the store.

Then in 1869 Bon Marché moved into stunning new purpose-built premises in the rue de Sevres. Imagine how you might have felt the first time you walked through the huge iron and glass doors and into its fabulous interior. Just imagine that thrill: stunning clothes, awe-inspiring furniture, drapery from all corners of the earth, sweets like you have never seen before, foodstuffs to make the mind boggle and baffling new gadgets that you cannot begin to fathom the workings of. You see assistants bustling here and there, catwalk displays of clothes and dressed mannequins among showman demonstrating the latest wonder. Every turn holds something new, a surprise, a wondrous assault to the senses. Imagine too how amazing it felt as you discovered that every department, as well as showing you awesome delights you'd never knew existed, had lots of nice things in them that you could afford. Bon Marché changed its ranges constantly, new surprises were guaranteed all the time. It's a product mix and stock management philosophy that worked then and still holds true today.

The concept of browsing a store was alien to the masses before 1852. It just was not a part of the contemporary ritual of shopping. Today browsers are essential to everyone from Wal-Mart through to Harrods. That's why we pack our stores with hot spots and why we change things so often. It's all down to Bon Marché and their astonishing nineteenth century Parisian innovations.

Picture: Koworld

Take a look at your shop through a kid's eyes; what can you make amazing?

So Bon Marché put surprise and delight at the centre of retail. It has remained there ever since. Surprise is one of the most important revenue-generating tools you have at your disposal. Surprise is about delivering on a customer expectation. What are customers doing when they browse your store? They are subconsciously demanding that you divert their attention. They are crying out for you to put that perfect pair of shoes under their nose. They are insisting that an unmissable recipe leaps out at them. Here's a wonderful thing: Paco Underhill, author of *Why We Buy* (2000), over years of watching has proven that customers, if they buy anything, almost always buy the first thing they pick-up. Surprise makes people touch things. Make a customer say 'wow' in your store and you've got a sale.

Suprise is about delivery on a customer expectation.

Case Study 11.1 Surprise at Selfridges

Selfridges was already two years into a significant transformation plan when they appointed Vittorio Radice as chief executive. Here was an inspirational leader, a romantic and a man with the golden age of the grand department store filling his head. Above all he recognized the value of surprise and wonder, he recognized the power of these emotions to fuel sales and profits.

In the mid-1990s however his was a vision not shared with the majority of department store corporate owners, Selfridges itself was under the wing of the moribund old stager Sears until 1998.

Many in the industry thought Vittorio was mad when he let the leashes off his buyers. Those buyers went creatively crackers dotting the store with esoteric oddities: £3000 sculptures, £10,000 dining tables, suits no one in their right mind could justify buying. Indeed a TV documentary of the time enjoyed poking fun at Vittorio and his newly creative store.

Retail analysts began to get seriously cold feet when the team then invested millions in ripping out and renovating the store's central escalators. They were shocked that the store would lose so much vital square footage for so long. But all the while that the press and analysts were nervously watching, Radice was also looking to the store fundamentals: fixing basic product mix issues, taking the dust off the merchandising, engaging the marketing team to reclaim the reputation of Selfridges as a 'house of brands'. He had the team creating a place to go for a treat – exciting, stylish, competitive retail therapy for customers.

A new energy swept through the store. The combination of new image, shocking and innovative ranges catering all the way through and beyond value, and a physically upgraded store space, all contributed. But for my money, above all else, the most effective element of Vittorio Radice's Selfridges transformation was the reintroduction of surprise. Customers were once again surprised, shaken even, challenged and delighted. After ten dull years an inspired Selfridges once again became a place to visit just for a treat, a nice place to browse, just for the hell of it 'oh and what if I happen to come away with a nice designer shirt?'

Sales climbed, margins improved and the store is once again a place of excitement and delight. Department store pioneer and visionary Gordon Selfridge himself would have been proud. Radice has moved on to pastures new but has clearly left a team in place who share his exciting romantic vision of what great department stores should be.

Making surprise work for you

How do you successfully introduce surprise into your store?

Here are some ideas

▶ Ensure you bring in a steady flow of new products.

▶ Use lighting and music to create drama in the store.

▶ Get the team to talk to customers and direct them to new and exciting products, promotions or events.

▶ Introduce a calendar of in-store demonstrations, events, and 'how to's – bring the theatre of retail into your store.

▶ Make use of 'manager's specials' and clearance items – many managers avoid being, as they see it, lumbered with such products, don't be! They are a customer honey pot if used correctly. Merchandise clearance lines are attractive to customers some of whom will even begin to make special visits to you just to check what you've got this week. The tip here is to take everything you can (independents must be a little more selective but do remember to talk to reps and agents about such lines), ship the real grot back to the manufacturers for a credit and make an honest promotion out of the remaining items. You know you could even argue that the merchandise strand of the world's most profitable retailer (profit/square foot) Richer Sounds is founded on creative marketing of clearance lines.

▶ Think like a customer – what would 'wow' me?

Epilogue
Bloody hell, what just happened?

You're here! You finished it! I hope you enjoyed reading *Smart Retail* as much as I did writing it. This is a practical book and I would like to think that you are out there putting this stuff into practise as we speak. Please tell me what you thought about *Smart Retail*. I would especially like suggestions for improvements and news of how using *Smart Retail* in the wild has worked out for you.

Further *Smart Retail*

Smart Retail speaking

Smart Retail wants to come to your conference, to your event and to your managers – we offer a high-energy, practical talk that sends delegates away buzzing with ideas.

Smart Retail seminars

Seminars that work – delivering to your managers a new stream of practical ideas, proven strategies and retail techniques that will help them to win the daily sales battle.

Smart Retail consultancy

Practical consultancy for real world performance improvement.

Thank you for buying and reading *Smart Retail*.
All the best,
Richard.

My e-mail address is richard@retailkings.com or see more at www.retailkings.com.

Appendices

A   Team meetings

B   My favourite retailers

C   Books for retailers

D   Bibliography

Appendix A Team meetings

I recommend you hold a fifteen minute team meeting every day. Now, you don't have to do this but all the best retailers do. It's hard to build a team spirit if the team never gets to stop to spend a few minutes focusing together. Equally what better way is there to swap ideas, to jump on to opportunities and to share responsibilities?

Daily team meetings are the missing ingredient in many otherwise great store manager's repertoire. In your store diary write into the top of tomorrow's date the items that you want to talk about in the next day's team meeting. Some of the items worth covering in these meetings include:

▶ customer service issues and how these were solved

▶ forthcoming events

▶ promotions

▶ new products just in

▶ bargains identified

▶ review competitor activity

▶ review new best practice ideas identified

▶ discuss incentive schemes

▶ review any challenges

▶ introduce new employees

▶ review targets and performance

▶ celebrate success

▶ recognition

▶ consider improvement ideas – even if you can only do this one, it will have been worth having the meeting.

Appendix B My favourite retailer

There is no science in this appendix and I'm not really sorry for that! This is a list of my heroes. These are the retail brands that I've picked out as being among the most important to have ever opened their doors. I've made the majority of selections from present day rather than way back, that way you can actually have a wander around them and decide if you agree with me or not.

To uphold impartiality, I've only listed brands that I have never worked for. I expect my clients will stop sending me Christmas cards as a result. I've also left off some great names that I don't really know enough about to put in the list. Giants such as Promodes, Ahold and Federated are obviously terrific retailers but I've never been close enough to them to really be sure of why.

So anyway here it is, in alphabetical order; my list of the World's greatest retailers.

Table B.1 World's greatest retailers

Who	When	Where	Why	Smart awards
amazon	1990s – 2000s	US	The website is as real a store as one you walk into. amazon changed the way books and CDs were sold off-line as well as on-line. It is easy to use hindsight to claim that amazon was just about the first to use new technology in a new way, but that misses the point. The principles that make amazon great: choice, bargains, surprise, awesome customer service, apply to any retail business. Jeff Bezos, brilliant founder of amazon, deserves credit for identifying the specific benefits of an Internet-based sales channel but equally he should be held-up as an example of a brilliant instinctive merchant too.	
Bhs	1990s – 2000s	UK	Philip Green bought the foundering Bhs during the 1990s and turned it around so comprehensively that it is now one of the UK's most profitable	UK's Smartest Retail turnaround

Table B.1 Continued

Who	When	Where	Why	Smart awards
			retail businesses. Look around the store and you can see why, they know their customer and they give that customer what he/she wants. Well-made nice things at a fair price. All flab and unnecessary cost has been stripped out of the company too. It is a combination that is obvious but so often missed.	
Bon Marché	1860s	France	Astride and Marguerite Boucicaut were the retail visionaries who created the concept of the department store. They saw shops as grand theatre; palaces of spending. They even had dramatic architects such as Gustave Eiffel (who designed the Eiffel tower and who engineered the inside of the Statue of Liberty) involved in creating the fabric of their store.	
Boots	2000s	UK	It's a chemist's but people like to go to Boots to browse and find treats – that's awesome when you stop to really think about it.	
Carphone Warehouse	1990s – 2000s	UK	In a market characterised by poor service and worse, this brand is a beacon of honesty and service excellence. They really look after staff too and it shows when you shop the store.	
Cash Converters	2000s	Australia	'A better way to sell, a great place to shop' that's the tag-line of this brilliant franchised pawn broking (they prefer the term second-hand store) business. These shops trade from cheap locations, generate very high traffic and turn stock very fast. It is a genius concept brilliantly executed, what is shows is the value of trade-in for building store traffic. Every store that can feature trade-ins absolutely must embrace the concept.	

Table B.1 Continued

Who	When	Where	Why	Smart awards
Habitat	1970s – 80s	UK	I find it hard to decide if Terence Conran is a genius or was just lucky to have great teams around him. Whatever, the Habitat shops he created, now owned by Ikea, really did change British habits in some important ways. Duvets are the classic example; the popularity of duvets is directly down to Habitat. They introduced them to the UK and made a big fuss of the fact that duvets represented freedom from the old household chores like making the bed, and freedom from bed being only a place to sleep. Beds became fun. That was typical of what made this store great. Habitat was prepared to challenge customers and then to stick to its convictions. More often than not it won through in the end. After all, when, other than in a chintzy hotel, did you last sleep in a bed under old fashioned sheets? Habitat is one of the rare examples of a retailer successfully anticipating customers' future needs and then meeting those needs now. Tough one to pull off but am I glad that such innovators exist. Hats off to Conran.	
IKEA	1940s – 2000s	Sweden	The story of why IKEA customers go into a warehouse area to pick-up their furniture is a great illustration of why this company is a great one. In the early days of IKEA you didn't do that, a helper went and found your stuff for you. Then in 1965 they opened a big new store in Stockholm and the first day sales went crazy. There were more customers than the store could handle. Things were awful at the collection area. So the IKEA manager made a judgement call, he opened-up the warehouse and allowed customers to come in and find their own items. It worked so well that they tried it again and the rest is history. In IKEA, that manager was recognized for having improved the way the store worked. Anywhere else and he'd have been	World's Smartest Retailer

Table B.1 Continued

Who	When	Where	Why	Smart awards
			sacked for breaking the rules. Ingvar Kamprad is the visionary who created IKEA in 1943. His guiding philosophy came to be 'A better life everyday for the majority of people'. I think he meant it too. IKEA is much more than the generation of profits. It offers good things to lots of people at a low cost and without class distinctions. It is accessible, exciting and honest. In 1976 Kamprad wrote his seminal retail manifesto *Testament of a Furniture Dealer*. In it you read statements such as 'to make mistakes is the privilege of the active person. Only while asleep does one make no mistakes' and 'an idea without a price tag is unacceptable'. That character is strong in IKEA all over the world. It is so strong that it can be made to cross cultural borders. IKEA in Croydon is as recognizable in its IKEA-ness as IKEA in Gothenburg. This is the best retail company to have ever opened its doors to a customer.	
Marks & Spencer	1970s – 80s	UK	The rise, fall and rise again of Marks' is well documented. Despite that very rocky middle patch M&S remains one of the world's best ever retailers. During the first strong period its success was driven by an unrivalled product range that perfectly reflected the everyday needs of its customers. Clothes especially were always well made and quality was an essential added-value attraction. Dependability was another important aspect of the story. Customers felt they could depend on M&S to sell to them well-made products that met their needs and occasionally exceeded them. Marks & Spencer is a different company today but having listened to customers and staff it is strong once again.	
Next	1980s	UK	Launched by the brilliant George Davies. He took the moribund old Hepworths stores and turned them into the	

Table B.1 Continued

Who	When	Where	Why	Smart awards
			absolute clothing icon of the 1980s. Next was home to every aspirant yuppie, me included. These were well-made clothes at an affordable price, cut in classic styles. The clothes and the branding fit the mood of the day perfectly. Davies is an absolute retail legend, one of my personal retail heroes. His George at Asda value clothing range and the 2001-launched Per Una brand are also runaway sales success stories. George also owns a pub in the Cotswolds and can sometimes be found serving customers behind its bar; incredible!	
Ottakar's	2000s	UK	Ottakar's founder James Heneage loves books. He employs other people who love books. And it shows; you can feel the staff's enthusiasm for books every time you walk in the stores. That translates directly into excellent customer service and an enjoyable customer experience. What most attracts me to the Ottakar's story though is their location strategy. Now this is of course usually a pretty dull, though vital, area of retail. But what this chain has successfully delivered is a strategy of serving the small towns and avoiding the major High Streets. Bigger fish in smaller ponds effectively. It was a brave move and it suits the feel of the stores; local, friendly, and independent. That's a neat trick for a national chain to pull off. Oh, and in case you were wonding; Ottakar's is named after King Ottokar from the *Tintin* books. So there you go.	
Richer Sounds	1990s –	UK	Guinness Book of Records holder for highest sales/square-foot of any retailer anywhere in the world. Have held this record for 11 years to 2003. Regularly features as the top UK-owned employer in the *Sunday Times* annual 'Best Companies to Work For' awards. Founder Julian Richer is in this for his employees as well as himself and that	UK's Smartest Retail employer

Table B.1 Continued

Who	When	Where	Why	Smart awards
			shows in everything they do. Go in and talk to any member of his team and then compare them with your own. What you are seeing is the reward retailers get when they treat their people with respect. A great, great business.	
Selfridges	2000s	UK	I've gone on a bit about Selfridges but that is only because it is so wonderful. I wish I worked for them!	World's most exciting Smart Retailer
Starbucks	2000s	US	The most consistently traded retail brand on Earth. A Starbucks in Paris is identical in every way to one in London or Seattle. These stores are even more consistent than McDonalds. This is one store where surprise isn't needed, customers love to know that whatever city they are in they can get the same great latte grande and the same strawberry/white-chocolate muffin. That reliability and predictability sells coffee.	
Target	2000s	US	Discount variety stores made funky. These stores are cheap but very hip, it's a superb achievement and proves that low ticket prices do not have to mean cheap and nasty product or stores.	
Tesco	1980s – 2000s	UK	Do you remember what we all thought of Tescos in the 1970s? A bit naff? First Lord MacLaurin and then Sir Terry Leahy turned that image around, they took the brand upmarket but without sacrificing the ability to provide good food at low prices. They attribute the turnaround to an incredible business-wide focus on company mission. Everything they did supported the aim of winning over customer's support in an honest fashion. After decades of holding second place, Tesco won the UK market share race and still hold that number one position.	

Table B.1 Continued

Who	When	Where	Why	Smart awards
			Incidentally, founder Sir Jack Cohen's autobiography *Pile It High* is a great read if you're interested.	
The Container Store	2000s	US	This one was a tip from George Whalin and what a store it is! They sell storage solutions – stuff to put stuff in. That's it. But they do it so brilliantly – walk into the Container Store and ask any member of staff for their thoughts on your particular storage challenge and you actually get proper advice. Ideas you can use and that have a real impact on your life at home. Those staff are among the best trained in retail too. In your first year with them you would receive 235 hours of training. The average in retail is below ten.	World's Smartest Specialist Retailer
TK/TJ Maxx	1990s – 2000s	US	How many times have you seen it 'kick off' in a TK Maxx? A shop that can have customers brawling over a T-shirt or a pair of jeans is getting something very right! Bargains, bargains, bargains coupled with surprise, surprise and more surprise is the key to this off-price apparel (US term – means branded clothes at clearance prices) store's incredible success.	World's Smartest Bargain Retailer
Toys 'Я' Us	1980s – 2000s	US	Took the traditional small toyshop and made it massive. This is a great example of specialism taken to the n'th degree. Why go anywhere else when everything you need is in one place? That's a powerful added-value proposition.	
Wal-Mart	1962 – 2000s	US	Sam Walton, the founder of Wal-Mart, is a total customer genius. More than that; in creating the world's biggest company he also showed how to create a consistency of culture that is truly amazing. Every single member of the worldwide Wal-Mart team knows exactly what the company does, how it should do it and why. The stores are packed with bargains, dependable value and lots of things to make customers smile.	World's All-time Smart Retailer

Table B.1 Continued

Who	When	Where	Why	Smart awards
Woolworths	1960s – 70s	UK	Woolworths was an essential store in the 1960s and '70s. It provided ordinary families, like mine, with nice things at a very low price. The quality was reliable and the range mind-blowing, some 70,000 different lines by the start of the 1980s.	

Appendix C Books for retailers

Decent books on retailing are few and far between, which is one of the reasons why I wrote this one. Of those rarities these are the best. Two of the titles are pretty hard to get hold of in the UK but are available over the web at www.amazon.co.uk. Good bookshops may be able to order them for you too. I've marked the two in question with asterisks.

The Richer Way – Julian Richer (Richer Publishing, 4th ed. 2001)

Richer manages people better than anyone I have ever come across. This is the story of how he does that – essential reading.

Why We Buy – Paco Underhill (Touchstone, 2000)

Retail anthropologist Underhill has an understanding of the habits of shopping that is just breathtaking.

Marketing Judo – John Barnes and Richard Richardson (Prentice Hall Business, 2003)

The successful duo behind the Harry Ramsden's phenomenon offer lots of ideas for building a business using brains rather than budget – lots that is relevant to owners of retail stores.

Retail Success – George Whalin (Willoughby Press, 2001)*

George worked in a famous guitar store in 1960s California and has been a leading retail mind ever since. He told me that the moment he realized that he wanted to be a retailer was the first time he sold a customer a guitar package that made both him and the customer smile. I love that.

The Beermat Entrepreneur – Mike Southon and Chris West (Prentice Hall Business, 2002)

If you don't yet have a store, or having read *Smart Retail* you feel you would rather set up on your own, then the unique methods described here offer a great way to make that dream real.

Made in America, My Story – Sam Walton (Bantam Books, 1992)*

The story of how Sam Walton and his team built the world's biggest company: Wal-Mart. This is a lot of fun, full of breathtaking daring, down-home philosophy and some great retail stories. An absolute must have.

Appendix D Bibliography

Blanchard, Kenneth H. (1983) *The 1-Minute Manager*. New York: Berkley Publishing Group.

Corina, Maurice *Pile It High*. London: Weidenfeld & Nicolson.

Peters, Tom and Austin, Nancy K. (1989) *A Passion for Excellence*. New York: Warner Books.

Richer, Julian (2001) 4th ed. *The Richer Way*. London: Richer Publishing.

Richer manages people better than anyone I have ever come across. This is the story of how he does that – essential reading.

Southon, Mike and West, Chris (2000) *The Beermat Entrepreneur*. London: Prentice Hall Business.

If you don't yet have a store, or having read *Smart Retail* you feel you would rather set up on your own, then the unique methods described here offer a great way to make that dream real.

Spotlight annual publication. London: Spotlight Publications.

Taylor, Don and Smalling-Archer, Jeanne (1994) *Up Against the Wal-Mart*. New York: Amacom.

Underhill, Paco (2000) *Why We Buy*. NY: Touchstone.

Retail anthropologist Underhill has an understanding of the habits of shopping that is just breathtaking.

Walton, Sam (1992) *Made in America, My Story*. NY: Bantam Books.*

The story of how Sam Walton and his team built the world's biggest company: Wal-Mart. This is a lot of fun, full of breathtaking daring, down-home philosophy and some great retail stories. An absolute must have.

Whalin, George (2001) *Retail Success*. CA: San Marcos: Willoughby Press.*

George worked in a famous guitar store in 1960s California and has been a leading retail mind ever since. He told me that the moment he realized that he wanted to be a retailer was the first time he sold a customer a guitar package that made both him and the customer smile. I love that.

Index